Nabia Abbott was born in Turkey in 1897. As a young child she was taken by her family across the Middle East to India, where she was educated in British schools and remained until after the first world war. Later she lived in Iraq and finally in the United States, where in 1933 she became the first woman faculty member of the Oriental Institute of the University of Chicago. A leading scholar of Arabic, she was a specialist in deciphering early Islamic papyri. She was the author of seven books and dozens of magazine articles. Nabia Abbott died in 1981.

Nabia Abbott

Saqi Books

Aishah—
The Beloved of
Mohammed

With a preface by Sarah Graham-Brown

British Library Cataloguing-in-Publication Data
A catalogue record for this book is available from the British Library

ISBN 0 86356 007 5 (pbk)

First published by the University of Chicago Press, 1942

This edition first published 1985 by Saqi Books
Reprinted 1998

Saqi Books
26 Westbourne Grove
London W2 5RH

Nabia Abbott (1897–1981)

Sarah Graham-Brown

For those today who are concerned with the position of women in the Muslim world, this account of the life of Aishah, the best-known of Mohammed's wives, may at first sight seem little more than a curiosity. Certainly from a feminist point of view its language seems archaic, presenting women in terms usually used by men. Yet the book—and its author—must be seen in the context of their time.

Aishah was written in 1942, in the middle of World War II and the latter years of the era of colonial rule in the Middle East. The early women's movement, particularly in Egypt, had already begun to make its mark on society.

Those who support the women's movement in the Islamic world today often express the view that Islam, in its basic tenets, is favourable to the notion that women should have equal, or at least comparable, rights with men. According to this argument, it was the later development of restrictive traditions and social practice that 'distorted' Islam and led to systematic forms of oppression of women.

It is possible to cite portions of the Koran to support this view, as it is possible to justify a more restrictive interpretation. In recent years this issue has surfaced in a number of countries—in Egypt and Algeria in debates over the Personal Status Law and the Family Code respectively, and in Kuwait over the issue of women's political rights.

In this context, *Aishah* makes a useful contribution to the historical debate and its contemporary interpretation. Though the author's portrayal of women sometimes sounds inappropriate to present-day readers, in her own time Nabia Abbott's writings were breaking new ground. As she comments in her preface, this was, to her knowledge, the first full-length biography of Aishah. She adds that Orientalist scholars' interest in Aishah had been 'far too secondary' and had only highlighted in passing colourful incidents from her life.

But Abbott makes it clear that her other reason for writing this biography was the interest which the life of this lively and resourceful woman held for what she describes as 'the progressives of East and West'. Her discussion of the social and political position of Aishah and other women of that era was not intended as a mere exercise in scholarly exegesis of the Koran, nor as a sifting of the traditions about Aishah. It was part of a wider discussion in her work of the position of women in early Islam and its implications for the contemporary world.

For all that, Nabia Abbott was, in the eyes of her contemporaries, first and foremost a scholar. This alone makes her an unusual figure. In 1933 she became the first woman member of the Oriental Institute of the University of Chicago, and in 1963 she was made Emeritus Professor. In a tribute published in the Institute's 1974/5 annual report, Dr Muhsin Mahdi, formerly professor of Arabic and chairman of the university's Department of Near Eastern Languages, commented on 'the discrimination I knew she had faced as a professional woman in those pre-liberation days', and lists her major achievements as 'her pioneering work on the position of women in the Islamic Middle East; her classic study of the rise of the North Arabic script; her massive, painstaking, and path-breaking investigations of Arabic literary papyri, which have already revolutionized the study of the culture of early Islam; . . .'

Abbott's early life seems to have been one of constant movement. She was born in Mardin, in south-western Turkey, on 31 January 1897. Her father was a trader and, while she was still a child, she travelled with her family in a covered wagon in a caravan to Mosul and sailed down the Tigris to Baghdad. The family subsequently moved on to settle in Bombay. It was in India that Abbott received most of her education, attending English schools; during World War I she took a BA degree at Lucknow's Isabella Thorbom College for Girls, graduating in 1919. After the war she spent a brief period in Iraq, where she was involved in the establishment of a women's education programme, a subject that continued to interest her in later years.

Her family then moved to the United States, where she accompanied them and took her masters degree at Boston University, graduating in 1925. She subsequently became first a faculty member and then head of the history department at Asbury College in Wilmore, Kentucky, where she remained until 1933.

When her family moved to Chicago in that year she went to work under Martin Sprengling, professor of Arabic at the Oriental Institute, and began her career there with a study of the Institute's collection of rare early Islamic documents. In order to do this, she immersed herself in the history of early Islamic society, out of which grew her interest in the position of women in that society.

The biography of Aishah (1942) was one of two full-length works she wrote on the subject, the other being *Two Queens of Baghdad* (1946), a biographical portrait of Khaizuran and Zubaidah, respectively mother and wife of Harun al-Rashid, the most celebrated caliph of the Abbasid period.

In both these works her prime concern seems to have been to retell history giving weight to the influence of outstanding women. In general this influence was exercised through men, an exception being the later years of Aishah's life, after the death of Mohammed, when she sought to play a direct and independent role in politics.

Sometimes, in *Aishah,* Abbott seems overly cautious in her analysis of events and occasionally seems unwilling to speak out explicitly on issues of religious practice and women's role which emerge in the narrative. Some contemporary writers on women in the Middle East have criticized this caution. The other weakness of the book from a contemporary point of view is the language she uses to describe her female characters, and particularly relationships between men and women. She sometimes seems to have deliberately sought to achieve a tone appropriate to the romantic novels of the day, probably in an effort to reach a wider audience than in her strictly scholarly works. Nonetheless, by introducing women as actors in the life and power struggles of early Islam, and not as mere appendages of men, she contributes to a broadening of historical perspective which even now is refreshing and stimulating.

Her mainly narrative biographical works are complemented by her more analytical general essays and articles on the subject of women in pre-Islamic society and in early Islam. 'Women and the State in Early Islam', published, like *Aishah*, in 1942 (*Journal of Near Eastern Studies* I: pp. 106–26, 341–68), paints a broader picture and makes explicit some of the arguments that do not always come into clear focus in the biography.

Here she addresses the question of the effects of early Islam on women in terms of both the example provided by Mohammed's own life and the institutionalization of Islam after his death. Although Abbott essentially supports the view that the position of women grew progressively more circumscribed after Mohammed's own day, she argues that there were aspects of his own actions and pronouncements which laid the basis for limits on women's freedom that turned out to be more severe than those which had existed in pre-Islamic days.

But she also takes the view that later restrictions were more the result of socio-economic changes in the rapidly expanding Islamic empire than the consequence of religious tenets as such. It was their interpretation in the light of particular social conditions that was more significant.

In Mohammed's own attitude to women she detects two sometimes contradictory strands. One was a willingness to initiate certain reforms—for instance the ending of female infanticide—while adopting a generally piecemeal and *ad hoc* approach to the whole question of women's rights. Often, she says, he was responding to particular local situations 'calling for a comparatively prompt decision rather than the product of the deep and far-sighted thought of a legislator weighing in the balance abstract principles and ideals of human conduct'.

'It is safe to state', she asserts, 'that Mohammed avoided drastic innovations and that he tolerated and adopted such public and private practices as had become well established through long usage, provided these were reasonably compatible with the cardinal doctrine of monotheism and the requirements of a theocratic state' (p. 106). She contends that Mohammed therefore accepted 'the honoured position that the free Arab woman had enjoyed in pre-Islamic Arabia'. This of course must be distinguished from the position of women who were slaves or freed slaves.

But she points out that while Mohammed did initiate some improvements in the economic and legal status of all Muslim women, other aspects of his practice 'left woman forever inferior to man, placed one step below him' (p. 107). She ascribes this in part to the effects of his decision to take a large number of wives, for both political and personal reasons. This, as the narrative of *Aishah* shows, led to considerable complications in his domestic affairs towards the end of his life, and to his decision to seclude his wives. While this practice apparently was not widely followed during those early years, it set a precedent for the future.

But more crucially she examines the actual status of women in public life in the early days of Islam, arguing that 'it was during this period that the seeds of definite politico-religious discrimination against women were sown' (p. 107).

In the religious domain, women were readily accepted by Mohammed as converts and received encouragement and even honours. But as Abbott points out, the 'crucial test of woman's real position is to be looked for in the field of active leadership. Was she allowed to fill all or any of the public offices associated with the new religious life?' (p. 111). Her answer is that while Mohammed generally made no objection to, for instance, a woman acting as a prayer leader in her own household, even for both sexes, he did not particularly encourage it and in fact women seldom held any significant public religious position. Although after his death his wives, and particularly Aishah, as 'Mothers of the Believers' were able to exert considerable influence, the role of women in the public aspects of religion rapidly diminished.

'Even if Mohammed was, at first, disposed to allow active religious leadership among the women, later, partly because of some personal episodes in his life, he initiated the principle and practice of seclusion, with his wives setting the example. This and the fact that [the caliph] Umar ibn al-Khattab was opposed to public participation by women crystallized in the period under consideration [the reigns of the first four caliphs] the Moslem woman's orthodox position into one of passivity and submissiveness comparable to that already imposed on the women of her Jewish and Christian neighbours' (p. 115).

In the domain of politics, not suprisingly, Abbott finds the situation still 'less encouraging'. While there were still notable women, Aishah included, who wielded considerable influence and even fought in battles, they could seldom act directly, rather being obliged to seek influence through fathers, husbands, brothers, or sons. Abbott argues that while Aishah's part in the Battle of the Camel (in the year 656) demonstrated that some men were willing to follow the lead of a woman, her defeat and consequent retirement from public life was a setback for her in particular and for women in general.

She notes that at this time a tradition ascribed to Mohammed surfaced in which, remarking the fact that a woman was on the throne of Persia during the final struggle between the Persian empire and Byzantium, he said that 'a people who place a woman over their affairs are unfortunate or unhappy or do not prosper'. Since this tradition first appears in connection with Aishah's civil war with Ali, Abbott considers it 'highly improbable' that Mohammed was responsible for it. However, the fact that it became current when a woman was playing an important part in political events was significant in itself, and boded ill for the future fortunes of women in politics.

Abbott therefore argues that over the first century and a half of Islam, women's freedom and influence in the new state were already in steady decline. She sees the moves towards the total seclusion of women of the new aristocracy mainly as the result of the rapid conquests of early Islam, which brought increased wealth and access to female slaves. The latter began to take on the role of concubines, with freeborn wives more and more frequently veiled and secluded 'for reasons of sexual jealousy and social prestige'. These women's links with the outside world thus became attenuated, which in turn made it harder for them to break out of their isolation. Ironically, only slave and bedouin women retained a greater degree of freedom of movement.

Under the influence of these trends, Abbott concludes, 'the royal harem [began] to take on some of the characteristics of a sumptuous female prison guarded by that tragic but sinister figure, the eunuch'.

In a later article, published in 1956 ('Women', in Ruth Nanda Anshen, ed., *Mid-East: World Center: Yesterday, Today and Tomorrow*; Science of Culture Series Vol. 7, New York 1956, pp. 196–212), Abbott approaches the history of women in Islam from the point of view of the contemporary world. She holds that in many respects the history of women's oppression under all three major monotheistic religions has been similar. 'The status of women in the Middle East has roots that reach back to pre-history. The same major forces controlled her destiny here as, until recently, in the West. Semitic religions and Aryan cultures joined forces to bend and mould her to man's will and desire.' . . . 'Equating physical with moral power, man toyed with the idea of his own superiority and willingly succumbed to the "immortal myth" of woman's inferiority . . .

'Judaism, Christianity and Islam turned myth into dogma on the basis of the biblical and Koranic story of the creation and the fall of Adam and Eve' (p. 196).

She argues that in all three religions essentially the same devices were used to keep women in a position of inferiority: 'the ever-present threat of physical violence too readily executed; energy- and time-consuming excessive child-bearing in the interest of passion, church, or state; denial of free access to the world of books and publications; psychological attitudes that undermine self-esteem and eventually induce in all but the strongest of body and mind a false and vicious inferiority complex' (pp. 198–99). Despite the strength of this condemnation, she defends medieval Islam against some of the misconceptions and oversimplifications of Orientalists in the West, where 'the term "harem" has come to connote everything vicious and to exclude everything wholesome in the relationships of the sexes' (p. 203). Furthermore, she points out that those in the West who, in the eighteenth and nineteenth centuries, began to give thought to the emancipation of women tended to point to Islam as embodying the ultimate in the degradation of women. This, she adds, brought 'denials and apologetics from the Muslim world' and claims of women's superior status under Islam. In her view, this reaction is almost as invidious as the Western claims are false.

Her attitude towards the women's movement in the Middle

East at that time radiates hope. She described the movement, with 'its far-reaching implications', as 'the most significant single factor in changing the Middle East, even as the status of woman is everywhere the most significant measure of civilization and human progress'. Seen from the perspective of the 1980s, her analysis seems poignantly over-optimistic, though she was clearly aware that progress towards equality was neither easy nor straightforward.

She judged that the twin factors which had allowed the women's movement, particularly in Egypt and Turkey, to develop and achieve a measure of success were access to education and participation of women in the nationalist struggle. What she was not able to see at that time were the limitations and weaknesses which would be revealed in both mass education and nationalist politics in lessening inequalities for women, and for society as a whole.

Equally, her view of the role of religion as a reforming influence on society along the lines of Muslim thinkers in Egypt such as Mohammed Abduh has proved wide of the mark. 'Apologetics and eclecticism have ever been effective tools of change in Islam, as in its sister faiths and cultures. The West should neither ridicule nor underestimate them, as some tend to do. Used in the current climate of reform, they hold much promise for progressive social action. Nor should one underestimate the will and power of Middle Eastern women to speed this action where the law has not yet caught up with evolving practice' (p. 211).

To

MOTHER

Preface

MOHAMMED, the prayerful and perfumed prophet of Islam, was avowedly a great lover of the ladies, for whom, in turn, he held no small attraction. He was definitely among that class of great men who have the good fortune to win and retain the energetic support and wholehearted devotion of some able and loving women who contribute largely to the success and pleasure of their lives. Of Mohammed's several wives, two—Khadījah and Aishah—had more to offer along these lines than any of the others.

The Quraish had been long dominant at Mecca. The most aristocratic and powerful branches of the tribe at the time of Mohammed were the Banū Umayyah and the Banū Makhzūm. The future prophet of Arabia, however, came from the then more or less obscure clan of the Banū Hāshim. Left an orphan, Mohammed was brought up for a while by his grandfather and then by his none too prosperous paternal uncle, Abū Ṭālib. He, therefore, had to apply himself early to the common task of earning a living. It was not until he, as a handsome and dreamy youth, had stirred the heart of his elderly but well-to-do employer—the widow Khadījah—that he had the opportunity to devote himself to his dreams. His marriage to Khadījah brought him freedom from economic care and leisure for spiritual contemplation. It brought him also the firm faith and energetic devotion of an able and enthusiastic woman. She became his first convert and ever staunch supporter in the face of determined and distressing opposition. She won, in return, a place in his affections that no other woman could ever usurp. Her death was one of the severest blows that struck the rejected prophet of Mecca.

The *Hijrah*, or Flight, of Mohammed to Medina in A.D. 622, was the first step in his finally successful mission. This success was reflected in the growing size of his harem of young girls and mature aristocratic women that now graced, now plagued, his private life. Between them, these brought him the enviable gifts of political alliances, social prestige, ravishing beauty, gay youth, and mature charm. Of this impressive collection, Aishah, the young and vivacious daughter of Abū Bakr—Mohammed's right-hand man and Islam's first caliph—made her way deeper than any of the rest into the much-engaged affections of the aging prophet. Khadījah, with her faith and support, had steadied Mohammed's troubled spirit on the threshhold of his prophetic career. Aishah, with her lively temperament and pert charm, brought a refreshing air of romance into the closing years of his life.

But Aishah, at Mohammed's death, still had the greater part of her own life ahead of her. How she made herself felt in the life of the prophet and how, after his death, she continued, for something like half a century, to exert her influence on the affairs of the new Moslem state are major and lively themes of early Islamic history. Outside the Islamic world, Aishah as the favorite wife of Mohammed is the most widely known of all Moslem women. Orientalists, whose interest in her has been far too secondary, have stopped here and there to highlight some spectacular event of her colorful life.

This, as far as I know, the first full-length biography of Aishah, was launched on its way partly by an urge to know and to make known more of the life of this First Lady of Islam and partly as a tribute to the new Moslem world. For progressive Moslems of today, be they Arab or Persian, Indian or Chinese, Mongol or Turk, not only are keenly interested in the problems of the current Moslem woman's movement but show a gratifying curiosity regarding the achievement of the historic women of Islam. Aishah, the most famous of this group, bids fair to be of special interest to the progressives of both East and West in a world so rapidly contracting.

The student of any phase of early Islam is confronted at the start with that vast body of generally little-read but much-condemned Islamic source material—tradition. The condemnation is largely but not wholly deserved. Tradition, it is true, has brought forth much tares among the wheat. But a good deal of the former is so evident that it can be readily weeded out. Among the rest, the discerning eye alights on patches of golden grain that should be gratefully harvested, even at the risk of gathering in a tare or two. For what garnering of any source of human history is ever entirely free from all risks? Besides, for the tedious task of much weeding, the cautious reaper is rewarded in another direction. These traditions, cast from the start in a conversational and anecdotal vein, have preserved certain human elements that all too frequently are lost sight of alike in meager annals and bulky systematized compilations.

The great danger of this particular Islamic source material lies in the indiscriminate use of isolated traditions or of groups of traditions emanating from single, biased sources or from well-defined politico-religious groups, each seeking to establish that version of "history" that best suited its claims and ambitions. But considerably heavy spade work has been done along the lines of critical research in early Islamic history to expose notorious individual fabricators of tradition and well-organized politico-religious camps expertly at work in the use of this tool as effective propaganda of all sorts and for any occasion. One needs but mention such scholars as Wellhausen, Goldziher, Nöldeke, Caetani, and even such extremists as Lammens and Casanova, to realize the great extent of the invaluable service rendered along these lines. The student who profits by this service ere he digs for himself into tradition need not rest from his labors empty handed. For within a reasonable margin of error he can learn to detect the true from the false and the probable from the improbable.

It is again my happy privilege to acknowledge my great indebtedness to Professor Martin Sprengling, who has been an ever inspiring and most generous colleague. He followed the development of the present study with constant and enthusiastic interest, reading each section as it was first completed. He gave liberally of his time and store of knowledge in making pregnant suggestions and pertinent criticisms. To the Oriental Institute and its director, Professor John A. Wilson, I am grateful for a subvention toward publication. Professor Wilson has, in addition, done me the great favor of reading the entire manuscript and offering many valuable suggestions. My thanks are also due to the University of Chicago Press for many and varied services in the course of publication.

Nabia Abbott

Oriental Institute
Chicago 1942

Contents

I

Beloved of Mohammed

HISTORY and tradition are overwhelmingly in favor of assigning the first place of influence in Mohammed's prophetic career, the earlier role of Khadījah excepted, to the first convert outside Mohammed's family, the lifelong and faithful friend, ʿAbd Allah ibn Abī Quḥāfah, famous for all time in the Moslem world as Abū Bakr al-Ṣiddīq. He and his family lived in the same quarter of the city of Mecca as did Khadījah and Mohammed. Here, in about A.D. 614, was born his daughter Aishah. She was given out for nursing and foster-parentage, as was the custom in Arabia, to a Makhzūmite family.[1] She is accounted by some as the nineteenth convert to Islam, which may mean nothing more than that she as a child was reckoned as a believer.[2] At any rate, she herself could not remember the time when both her parents were not Moslems and when Mohammed himself did not visit at her father's house morning

[1] Ibn Ḥanbal, *Musnad* (6 vols.; Cairo, 1313/1895–96), VI, 201, 33 and 38.

[2] Abū Zakariyā Yaḥyā al-Nawawī, *Kitāb Tahdhīb al-Asmā* ("Biographical Dictionary"), ed. Ferdinand Wüstenfeld (Gottingen, 1842–47), p. 849; Ibn Hishām, *Sīrah*, ed. Ferdinand Wüstenfeld (Gottingen, 1859), p. 163.

and evening.[3] Doubtless Mohammed had taken some notice of this lively girl-child of his "brother" in the faith. A touching story is told of how on one of these visits he saw the little Aishah at the door of her home crying bitterly. Affected by her tears, he sought to comfort the child and soon discovered that parental discipline was the cause of her distress. He gently rebuked the mother, Umm Rūmān, and, though she told him that Aishah had carried tales to Abū Bakr (which had roused his temper), yet Mohammed requested her to be gentle with the child for his sake.[4]

Though the advantages of a marriage between Mohammed and the family of Abū Bakr may have been early and readily evident to both parties, yet it seems that neither of them was the first to conceive the idea of a marriage between the elderly Mohammed and the child Aishah. Tradition generally credits a maternal aunt of Mohammed, Khawlah bint Ḥakīm,[5] with putting the idea into Mohammed's head. She was an early convert and the wife of that would-be ascetic, ᶜUthmān ibn Maẓᶜūn,[6] whom Mohammed took to task for his celibatic outlook on life and his neglect of Khawlah. Tradition reports that Khawlah served the prophet, which may mean that she sometimes took care of his simple household after Khadī-

[3] Ibn Saᶜd, *Ṭabaqāt* (9 vols.; Leiden, 1905–40), VIII, 54, and Ibn Ḥanbal, VI, 212; Bukhārī, *Ṣaḥīḥ*, ed. Krehl (4 vols.; Leiden, 1862–1908), IV, 131.

[4] Ibn Saᶜd, VIII, 54.

[5] *Ibid.*, p. 113; Ibn Ḥanbal, VI, 409.

[6] Ibn Saᶜd, III[1], 286–91; Ibn Ḥanbal, VI, 268 f.

jah's death. She was close enough to him to feel free to suggest that he marry again.

"Whom shall I marry, O Khawlah? You women are best knowing in these matters," answered Mohammed.

"If you wish a virgin, there is the daughter of him whom you love best, Aishah bint Abī Bakr; but, if you wish a nonvirgin, there is the widow Sawdah bint Zamᶜah who believed in you and followed you."

"Go," said Mohammed, "bespeak them both for me."

So Khawlah went on her congenial mission first to the house of Abū Bakr, where she broke the news to Aishah's mother who deferred the matter to her husband. Abū Bakr seemed a little uncertain as to the propriety or even legality of marrying his daughter to his "brother." Mohammed, however, hastened to ease Abū Bakr's mind by reminding him that they were brothers in faith only.[7]

But there was another obstacle in the way. Aishah, child though she was, had been already promised to a young relative named Jubair. The matter, therefore, had to be taken up with the youth's father, Muṭᶜam ibn ᶜAdī, whose family was still heathen. Abū Bakr went to see what he could do about it. No sooner did he touch on the subject than the youth's mother objected to the previous arrangement between them on

[7] Ṭabarī, *Tārīkh* ("Annales"), ed. de Goeje (15 vols.; Lugduni Batavorum, 1879–1901), I, 1768; Ibn Ḥanbal, VI, 210 f.; Bukhārī, III, 415; Ibn Ḥajar, *Kitāb al-Iṣābah* (Calcutta, 1873), IV, 691 f.

the grounds that she feared the marriage would lead to her son's conversion to Islam. Muṭᶜam seconded his wife's objection, and "thus did Allah release Abū Bakr from his promise."[8] Khawlah's matrimonial mission to Sawdah having also proved successful, Mohammed, within a few months of Khadījah's death in A.D. 619, married in quick succession the widow Sawdah and the six-year-old Aishah. The marriage of the latter, however, was not consummated until three years later in Medina.

The precocious child, if one is to believe the traditions attributed to her, sensed a change in her status when her mother called her away from her playmates and kept her indoors. She realized then that a marriage was involved but did not know to whom and would not ask; she waited instead on her mother to tell her.[9] There is no record of the child's reaction to the realization that she was to be the wife of the middle-aged prophet of Allah. For a while at least her main concern was the business of childhood play.

While Aishah's life in these last years at Mecca continued its childish tenor, her father Abū Bakr was wholeheartedly devoting his time, energy, and means to the prophet who was now his prospective son-in-law. It was to him that Mohammed confided his slowly maturing plans for the epoch-making *Hijrah*, or Flight, from Mecca to Medina. It was Abū Bakr's careful preparations and his quick action when Mo-

[8] Ibn Ḥanbal, VI, 211; Ibn Saᶜd, VIII, 39.

[9] Ibn Saᶜd, VIII, 40.

hammed finally announced Allah's authorization of the flight that made possible the successful execution of that hazardous venture. The child Aishah naturally played no part in these momentous events. Not so her courageous and ready-witted half-sister, Asmā, who stoutly denied any knowledge of her father's and Mohammed's whereabouts at the same time that she was secretly sending them provisions, some of which she herself took to the cave, near Mecca, in which the fugitives were hiding. Lacking some string either to tie up her packages or to let them down into the cave, she took off her girdle and tore it lengthwise to use as cords. It is from this incident that she came to be known in Moslem tradition as "she of the two girdles."[10]

Within a few weeks of their arrival at Medina, Mohammed and Abū Bakr made plans for their families to follow. Sawdah, Fāṭimah, and her sister Umm Kulthūm were led by Mohammed's adopted son, Zaid, who also took along his wife and son. Umm Rūmān, Aishah, and her sister Asmā were led by ᶜAbd Allah ibn Abī Bakr. Ṭalḥah ibn ᶜUbaid Allah—a cousin of Abū Bakr and one to figure frequently in Aishah's life—accompanied the group.[11] The journey was accomplished in unmolested safety. Sawdah and Mohammed's daughters were lodged with him; but the young Aishah stayed with her parents, first in a near-

[10] Ibn Hishām, p. 329; cf. Ṭabarī, I, 1235–41.

[11] Ibn Saᶜd, VIII, 43; Ṭabarī, III, 2439 f.

by house, and later in their home in the suburb of Sunḥ.

The months which followed were busy and critical ones for Mohammed and his followers, the *muhājirūn*, or "fugitives" of Mecca. They had to make a place for themselves in the new order without alienating or imposing too much on the accommodating but ambitious *anṣārs*, or helpers of Medina. The Mosque of the Prophet was yet in building. Adjoining it rose a number of small private apartments for the members of Mohammed's family. Presently Sawdah was established in one of these; but still Mohammed said nothing about bringing the young Aishah "home." Abū Bakr, perhaps a little uneasy, inquired of Mohammed the reason for this delay. On being told that it was Mohammed's inability to provide the marriage portion that prevented the consummation of the marriage, he proceeded forthwith to remove that obstacle by providing the marriage portion himself.[12] It is not clear just when the marriage actually took place. According to some versions, it was in the month of Shawwāl of the Year 1, that is, some seven or eight months after the arrival at Medina; but, according to others, it was not until after the Battle of Badr, that is, in Shawwāl of the second year of the *Hijrah*.[13]

In no version is there any comment made on the disparity of the ages between Mohammed and Aishah

[12] Ibn Saᶜd, VIII, 43; cf. Henri Lammens, "Le 'Triumvirat' ...," *Mélanges de la Faculté oriental*, IV (1910), 119 f.

[13] Nawawī, p. 849; Ṭabarī, I, 1263; cf. Caetani, *Annali dell' Islam* (10 vols.; Milan, 1905–26), I, 424.

or on the tender age of the bride who, at the most, could not have been over ten years old and who was still much enamored with her play. For, as she herself recounts, she and her playmates were out in the yard playing hard at their swing, when her mother or a group of women came and took her away, washed her face with a little water, and waited a while outside the door until the panting child regained her normal breathing. Then they went within where Mohammed sat surrounded by a company of men and women. Umm Rūmān, placing the child Aishah on his lap, gave the two her blessing by pronouncing an accepted marriage formula: "These are your family, may Allah bless you in them, and bless them in you."[14] The company took hasty departure. The playful child became the wife of the aging prophet of Allah. In later years, as Mohammed celebrated some of his subsequent marriages, Aishah would recall, with some envy and perhaps a little humiliation, her hasty marriage and the lack of any celebration in honor of that event.[15] She was now housed, like her "sister" Sawdah, in one of the apartments in the court of the mosque.

But, wife or no wife, she was at heart still a child, not yet ready to put away childish things. The elderly Mohammed understood and let nature take its course. Coming home, he would see his child-wife busy with her toys.

[14] Tirmidhī, *Ṣaḥīḥ* (13 vols.; Cairo, 1931–34), IV, 311.

[15] Ṭabarī, I, 1769 f., 1263; Ibn Ḥanbal, VI, 211.

"What are these, O Aishah?" he would ask.

"Solomon's horses," or "My girl-dolls," would come her unconcerned answer. Mohammed, smiling, watched her at play. On other occasions he would find her surrounded by her playmates, who, seeing him approach, would disperse or go into hiding, thus spoiling the play business of the day. But Mohammed, so Aishah herself tells us, would call these children together again and himself join in their games.[16] Once, when the *Ḥabashah*, or Abyssinians, were playing at war games in the court of the mosque, Mohammed, drawing her close to his side, allowed her to watch the entertainment for as long as she cared to stay, or, as she herself puts it, "until I had had my fill."[17] During a festival she had two maidens in her apartment entertaining her with their tambourines. Abū Bakr came in and sharply ordered them away. Mohammed hastened to the rescue with, "Let them be, O Abū Bakr; every people has its festivals and this is our feast day."[18]

As Aishah outgrew her dolls and little playmates, increasing the meanwhile in womanly grace and charm, she discovered in Mohammed an indulgent husband and in Abū Bakr a stern and ambitious father. But, as long as she and the aging Sawdah were the only wives of Mohammed, there was little occa-

[16] Ibn Saᶜd, VIII, p. 42; Ibn Ḥanbal, VI, 57, 166, 233.

[17] Ibn Ḥanbal, VI, 84 f., 166, 186 f., 233, 270.

[18] *Ibid.*, pp. 33 and 99.

sion for the vivacious Aishah to concern herself with jealous thoughts or for this still young wife to be called on by her father for direct personal service on his own behalf. This happy situation, however, was to be of brief duration. If Abū Bakr could see the advantage of a marriage alliance with Mohammed, there were doubtless others who could do the same with respect not only to Mohammed but also to other leading figures in the new community at Medina. The fiery ʿUmar ibn al-Khaṭṭāb, running teamed up with Abū Bakr, was not one to overlook his opportunities. His daughter, Ḥafṣah, had lost her husband at Badr. ʿUmar took the initiative to find her a suitable match, that is, one that should bring the plebeian ʿUmar social prestige or political power or both. He therefore approached the wealthy and socially esteemed son-in-law of the prophet, the Umayyad ʿUthmān ibn ʿAffān, who had recently lost his wife, Ruqaiyah—Mohammed's daughter—only to be told that ʿUthmān had no need of a wife. Frustrated here, he tackled Abū Bakr with the offer of Ḥafṣah's hand. Abū Bakr received the embarrassing honor with silence. Furious, ʿUmar hastened to Mohammed to complain of the insults he thought he had suffered. Mohammed, as usual, rose to the occasion.

"Shall I," he calmed his angry visitor, "lead you to a better son-in-law than ʿUthmān, and lead ʿUthmān to a better father-in-law than you?"

"Do so, indeed," ʿUmar answered readily.

"I will marry your daughter, and ʿUthmān shall

marry mine."[19] Thus was the threatened peace of the community preserved at the same time that Mohammed bound himself with closer ties to ᶜUmar, known also as ᶜUmar al-Fārūq, or the Separator (of the true from the false),[20] whose dynamic personality and driving power the prophet had rightly estimated.

What Abū Bakr's real feelings in this matter were, we perhaps will never know. He saw to it, however, that the powerful ᶜUmar bore him no grudge for the supposed insult. He hastened to explain that he had heard Mohammed speak of marrying Ḥafṣah and, not wishing to reveal Mohammed's plans, had for that reason kept quiet when ᶜUmar offered him her hand. Otherwise, he, Abū Bakr, would have certainly accepted Ḥafṣah.[21] It is readily to be seen that all parties concerned in this episode acted for political reasons. The marriage, which took place in Shaᶜbān of the Year 3 (January–February, A.D. 625), about a month before the Battle of Uḥud, placed Abū Bakr and ᶜUmar on a par as fathers-in-law of the prophet. It also gave Aishah her first serious harem rival—a young woman of some twenty years. Ḥafṣah's charms, however, proved no match for those of the lively Aishah; while her quick temper, for she was the true daughter of her father, had the opposite effect of Aishah's impudent but ready wit, which generally drew an

[19] Ibn Saᶜd, VIII, 56 f.; Balādhurī, *Ansāb*, V (Jerusalem, 1936), 7; *Iṣābah*, IV, 521.

[20] Ibn Saᶜd, III[1], 193 f.

[21] Ibn Saᶜd, VIII, 57 f.; Bukhārī, III, 431 f.

amused smile from the indulgent Mohammed. Their natural jealousies notwithstanding, the two co-wives, influenced by the political ties that drew their fathers into ever closer co-operation, found themselves, for the most time, working together. The older Ḥafṣah probably took the lead at first, for Aishah reports an incident that seems to fit best in this earlier period. Both girls were fasting one day when someone brought Ḥafṣah a meat dish with which she tempted Aishah to join her in breaking their fast. Later, when Mohammed came by, Ḥafṣah confessed, and the two sinners were told to substitute another fast day for the one they had broken. Aishah's later comment on Ḥafṣah's action was: "She was indeed the daughter of her father."[22]

Ḥafṣah's maid tells of another incident which may well belong in these earlier years of their comradeship. The two were visiting together when they saw the elderly Sawdah approaching. Inspired partly by envy of her economic prosperity, derived from her skill in the fine leather work of Ṭāʾif, they decided to play a mischievous prank on her. The coming of the fearful *dajjāl*, or false prophet, had been well impressed on the minds of the community, since the very thought of it would, on occasion, reduce Aishah to tears.[23] As Sawdah came within hearing distance, they cried out, "O Sawdah, are you not aware that the *dajjāl* has appeared?" Scared out of her wits, so the story goes, Sawdah ran to the nearest shelter, a

[22] Ibn Ḥanbal, VI, 141, 237 f., 263. [23] *Ibid.*, p. 75.

kitchen tent. The pranksters, choking with laughter, ran to share their joke with Mohammed. He hastened to the tent to reassure Sawdah, who emerged from her hiding-place covered with cobwebs and seemingly more relieved to find no *dajjāl* was on the scene than annoyed with her young rivals' practical jokes.[24]

The daughters of Abū Bakr and ᶜUmar, however, were soon to have more dangerous competition than the huge and aging Sawdah. In Ramaḍān of the Year 4, just over a year after his marriage to Ḥafṣah, Mohammed married another woman who, like Ḥafṣah, had been widowed at Badr. This was the generously inclined Zainab bint Khuzaimah, whose charities had already earned for her the title of *Umm al-Masākīn*, or "Mother of the Poor." She too was housed in one of the small apartments to the side of the mosque, but she was not destined to complicate for long the prophet's harem, for she died some eight months later.[25]

Mohammed's marriage to his fifth wife was quite a different matter. The new rival was the beautiful and proud Makhzūmite, Hind bint Abī Umayyah, better known as Umm Salamah.[26] Her husband, Abū Salamah, to whom she had borne several children, had been wounded at Uḥud but had recovered and continued to render good service until the wound broke out afresh and led to his death some eight months after Uḥud. Touching stories are told of Mo-

[24] *Iṣābah,* IV, 547.

[25] Ibn Saᶜd, VIII, 82.

[26] *Ibid.,* pp. 60–67 and 356; *Iṣābah,* IV, 885–90.

hammed's sorrow at the death of this faithful and valuable companion. Equally touching ones are told of the genuine affection that existed between Abū Salamah and his wife, Hind, who cried bitterly because her people, the Banū Mughīrah, refused to let her accompany her husband to Medina, until touched by her continuous grief they permitted her to leave Mecca to join him.[27] It was in Medina that she one day proposed to her husband that they make a covenant never to remarry after the other's death, wishing only to be united again in Paradise.[28] One would like to think that the proposition was made by a devoted wife who realized that her husband was likely to depart this world before her. Abū Salamah, however, was not to be outdone in generous consideration.

"Umm Salamah," he asked in answer, "will you obey me?"

"I never asked for your commands, without intending to obey them."

"When I die, remarry," came the order, followed by a prayer, "O Allah, grant Umm Salamah after me a better man than I, one that will give her neither sorrow nor pain."

After his death both Abū Bakr and ᶜUmar wished to marry her, but she declined the honor.[29] Mohammed too seems to have lost no time in presenting himself as a suitor. But the recently bereaved widow offered excuses.

[27] *Iṣābah*, IV, 886 f. [28] Ibn Saᶜd, VIII, 61.

[29] *Ibid.*, p. 62; Ibn Ḥanbal, VI, 317; *Iṣābah*, IV, 887.

"None of my people is here to consult with."

"As for your people, none of them absent or present would object to my suit," Mohammed assured her.

"I am advanced in age and have orphaned children."

"As for your age, I am older than you, and as for your orphans, they shall be the responsibility of Allah and his Messenger," Mohammed persisted.

"But I am a woman of an exceedingly jealous disposition, and you, O Messenger of Allah, acquire many women."

"As for that," came Mohammed's answer, "I shall pray Allah to uproot jealousy from your heart."[30]

Umm Salamah finally yielded. The marriage took place in Shawwāl of the Year 4 (March, A.D. 626), about a month after that of Zainab.[31] Aishah's reaction to this latest marriage of Mohammed is best told in her own words:

> When the Messenger of Allah married Umm Salamah, I was exceedingly sad, having heard much of her beauty. I was gracious to her, desiring to see her for myself. And, by Allah, I saw that she was twice as beautiful and graceful as she was reputed to be. I mentioned this to Ḥafṣah but she said, "No, by Allah, this is nothing but jealousy (clouding your vision); she is not as they say." Ḥafṣah too was gracious to her, and having called to see her, she said to me, "I see her not as beautiful as you say, not even anywhere near it; though she is (unquestionably) beautiful." I saw her afterwards and, by my life, she was as Ḥafṣah had said. But still I was jealous.[32]

[30] Ibn Saᶜd, VIII, 62 f.; Ibn Ḥanbal, VI, 317; *Iṣābah*, IV, 887 f.

[31] Ibn Saᶜd, VIII, 61.

[32] Ibn Saᶜd, VIII, 66; *Iṣābah*, IV, 888.

The introduction of the Makhzūmite Umm Salamah into the prophet's harem was to prove the beginning of a rift reflecting the ambitions of rival political factions.[33] Aishah and Ḥafṣah, acting as one in the interest of their fathers, represented the party in power. Umm Salamah leaned toward Fāṭimah and ʿAlī and, as Mohammed's harem increased, drew into her circle Ramlah bint Abī Sufyān, better known as Umm Ḥabībah, and Maimūnah bint al-Ḥārith, both of whom Mohammed married, primarily for political reasons, in the seventh year of the *Hijrah.*[34] Here, then, were reflected the earliest political parties in Islam. Aishah and Ḥafṣah represented the plebeian but powerful Abū Bakr and ʿUmar, who, having wholeheartedly launched and started Mohammed on a successful prophetic career, were ambitious to reap their rewards as heirs to his power. There was the aristocracy of Mecca represented by the Makhzūmite Umm Salamah and the Umayyad Umm Ḥabībah. There was finally the *ahl al-bait*, or legitimist party, with the timid Fāṭimah for its main hope and perhaps Maimūnah for a belated addition. With Aishah's party in power the other two, each opposed to or envious of it, found it convenient sometimes to unite their forces; though at other times their own specific ambitions and jealousies led them to go their separate way, as groups and even as individuals. The rest of Mohammed's wives, with no particular political axes

[33] Bukhārī, II, 126, 132 f.; cf. Lammens, *op. cit.*, pp. 121 ff.

[34] Cf. below, pp. 39 f.

of their own to grind, allowed their emotions or the demands of the hour to sway them now toward Aishah, now toward Umm Salamah. The most interesting and colorful of this group was Mohammed's next and sixth wife, Zainab bint Jaḥsh.

The story of Zainab's marriage to Mohammed, as told by most Western scholars, is one that gives most offense to Moslems the world over. These scholars use it generally to show to what great extent Mohammed had become the slave of sensual passion. The Moslems, in their turn, point to the Western treatment of the story to show to what extent racial and religious prejudice can carry scholars and missionaries away from the truth.[35] It is neither necessary nor desirable to detail here the differences, step by step, in the two points of view. The following seem to be the essential facts of the story: Zainab, granddaughter of ʿAbd al-Muṭṭalib and first cousin, on her mother's side, of Mohammed, had early migrated to Medina with the rest of her family. She does not seem to have been married, though she was at that time some thirty years of age and considered beautiful. Despite Zainab's reluctance, Mohammed arranged a marriage between her and his freedman and adopted son, Zaid ibn Ḥārithah, a former slave of Khadījah.[36] Little or nothing is heard of her until

[35] Cf., e.g., Maulvi Muhammad Ali, *The Holy Qur-án* (2d ed.; London, 1920), pp. 823 ff.; Muḥammad Ḥusain Haikal, *Ḥayāt Muḥammad* (Cairo, 1936), pp. 307 ff.

[36] Ibn Saʿd, VIII, 71 and 81; Baiḍāwī, *Anwār al-Tanzīl* . . . . , ed. Fleischer (2 vols.; Lipsiae, 1846–48), II, 129; Abū Nuʿaim, *Ḥilyat al-Awlīyā* . . . . (10 vols.; Cairo, 1932–38), II, 51 f.

several years later, when Mohammed, looking in vain for Zaid at his home, chanced instead to see Zainab in light disarray and went away murmuring, "Praised be Allah who transforms the hearts!" Zainab reported the incident to Zaid, who went to Mohammed and offered to divorce his wife should Mohammed wish to marry her. Mohammed, however, sent him away with, "Keep your wife and fear Allah." But for Zaid, humble in origin and unattractive in person, there was now no peaceful living with the haughty and ambitious Zainab, whom, therefore, he presently divorced. When the usual four-month period of waiting was over, Mohammed, on the strength of a specific permission from Allah, married Zainab. He now incurred the displeasure and criticism of the community, which considered the marriage incestuous, since in its code an adopted son had the same position and privileges as a real one. A new revelation silenced all criticism by declaring that an adopted son is never the same as a real son and by specifically permitting marriage with the divorced wife of an adopted son.[37]

It is not so much on these *facts* as it is on the *motives* behind them that the two groups mentioned above cannot be made to agree; and motives are seldom easy to trace or ferret out, even when dealing with a personality much less complex than that of Mohammed. Furthermore, the non-Moslem group generally judges the morality of both facts and motives from the more idealistic level of Western Christianity, while the Moslems view these in the light of

[37] Ibn Saᶜd, VIII, 71 f.; Baiḍāwī, II, 129 f.

the more practical level of the customs of Arabia of that day. It is, therefore, readily to be seen how one and the same Mohammed is condemned by the extremist of the one group as a voluptuary at the same time that he is revered by the extremist of the other group as a saint. Tor Andrae has done the most to narrow the wide gap between these two extreme points of view; for he not only claims but actually strives to paint an objective character delineation of the Arabian prophet with a cross-section of contemporary Arabian practices for an appropriate background. He thus comes the closest to seeing Mohammed the man as his believing contemporaries saw him. To these Mohammed was neither sinner nor saint but a man of like passions as theirs. And if Allah saw fit, in the matter of women, to grant Mohammed the prophet a few extra privileges denied to the common man and at the same time saw fit to use Mohammed's common-man passions as tools in the forging of a new order, then who were they, the common believers (who for the most time half-envied Mohammed), to question Allah's wisdom or pleasure in the matter?

And so the episode of Zainab came and passed, with Mohammed gaining rather than losing any prestige with the faithful. Zainab herself gladly joined Mohammed's household, boasting, as Aishah had feared, that Allah himself had arranged her marriage from above.[38] The marriage took place in the

[38] Ṭabarī, I, 1773.

month of Dhū al-Quᶜdah of the fifth year of the *Hijrah* (March–April, 627),[39] a short year after Mohammed's marriage to Umm Salamah. The young Aishah, in whose presence Mohammed had received the revelation permitting him to marry Zainab, had her misgivings and experienced new pangs of jealousy.[40] But this hardly more than thirteen-year-old girl-wife accepted the marriage as the will of Allah. For to Aishah and her "sisters" (except perhaps the two Jewesses, of whom more presently) Mohammed was as much a prophet as was Joseph Smith to "sister" Emma Hale or Brigham Young to "sister" Harriett Amelia Folsom of the Church of Jesus Christ of Latter-Day Saints. If any are inclined to question this or to scoff at these seventh-century Arab women's acceptance of the polygamous Mohammed as a prophet to their polygamous nation, let them recall the general situation that prevailed in the nineteenth-century American harems of these leaders of the Latter-Day Saints. Aishah recounts an incident which probably took place while she was still in her early teens. Mohammed, she relates, left her in charge of a captive of his. She, becoming preoccupied with the women, neglected to watch him carefully, and so he escaped. When Mohammed returned and found his captive gone, he was angered to the point of cursing Aishah with, "May Allah cut off your hand." He rushed out to order a search, and presently

[39] Ibn Saᶜd, VIII, 81; Ṭabarī, I, 1460–62.

[40] Ibn Saᶜd, VIII, 72.

the escaped man was recaptured. Returning home, Mohammed found Aishah anxiously looking her hands over.

"What is the matter with you, are you *jinn* possessed?" he asked.

"It is your curse," she answered. "I am looking to see which of my hands will be cut off." Mohammed, no doubt rebuked, praised Allah and asked forgiveness for his short temper and blessings on any man or women he may have cursed.[41]

Associated with Zainab's marriage to Mohammed is the introduction of the *ḥijāb*, or the seclusion "behind a curtain," for Mohammed's wives.[42] The most widely accepted story is that some of the wedding guests outstayed their welcome, thus causing Mohammed both inconvenience and annoyance. This brought on the revelation of the "Verse of the Curtain,"[43] which now runs as follows:

O ye who believe, enter not the houses of the Prophet, except when called to eat with him, without waiting his convenient

[41] Ibn Ḥanbal, VI, 52.

[42] Ibn Saᶜd, VIII, 124–26. For a recent and interesting discussion of the origins of the *ḥijāb* see Gertrude Stern, *Marriage in Early Islam* (London, 1939), chap. xiii. This work, entailing a great deal of conscientious labor on the part of the author, suffers, nevertheless, from an arbitrary limitation of the main sources to Vols. VIII and VI of Ibn Saᶜd's and Ibn Ḥanbal's works, respectively (see her Preface and Introduction). For example, on p. 115, n. 2, it is stated that the tradition associating the institution of the *ḥijāb* with Zainab's marriage is not to be found in Ibn Ḥanbal; as a matter of fact it is to be found in that work—not in Vol. VI, however, but in Vol. III, 105, 168, and 196.

[43] Sūrah 33:53; cf. Ibn Saᶜd, VIII, 74 f.; Bukhārī, III, 312 f.; Ibn Ḥanbal, III, 105, 168, 196.

time. But when ye are invited, then enter; and when ye have eaten, then disperse. And stay not for familiar discourse; for verily that giveth uneasiness to the Prophet. It shameth him to say this to you, but Allah is not ashamed of the truth. And when you ask anything of the Prophet's wives, ask it of them from behind a curtain; this will be more pure for your hearts and for their hearts. It is not fitting that you give any uneasiness to the Messenger of Allah or that you marry his wives after him ever; this verily would be a grievous thing before Allah.

The first part of the verse, dealing with seclusion, may have been given on this occasion. It is, however, extremely doubtful if the last part, that prohibiting the remarriage of Mohammed's wives, was given at that time or was originally a part of this verse.[44] Within some three years, from about the time of Zainab's marriage to about the eighth year of the *Hijrah*, Mohammed gave out a group of ordinances some of which affected the conduct of the Moslem women in general, but most of which related to the status and conduct of his own wives in particular. With the mass of contradictory traditions on hand, it is difficult to discover the chronological sequence of this series of regulations, since in most cases it is impossible to know with any certainty the time or the specific occasion for the formulation of the individual regulation in this group. It is, however, a mistake to assume that the bulk of these regulations curtailing women's liberties were motivated largely by Mohammed's personal passions, sexual or otherwise. There is sufficient indication that some at least can be

[44] See below, pp. 56–58.

traced back to the lax morals of Mohammed's generation.

One met in the Arabia of Mohammed's time several types of marriages, some of them with very loose ties. Polygamy was the rule and divorce the privilege of both sexes. Men could have as many wives as they chose, the heart and the purse setting the only limitations. Divorced women did not, as a rule, lack new husbands; some women are known to have married three and four times in succession.[45] Sex was nearly an obsession with the entire population, and sex talk, frank among the better element, tended to be indecent and lewd among the worst sort. Women, gayly attired, flaunted their charms and adornment, and men rose to the bait with open expression of admiration at the best and with insulting and insinuating offers at the worst. It is in the light of this background that Mohammed's ordinances affecting the conduct of the Moslem women must be viewed. In Sūrah 24:31–32 both believing men and believing women are "to cast down their looks and guard their private parts," while the women are further commanded to throw their head scarfs over their bosoms and to refrain from displaying their adornments except to such men as are within the prohibited degree of marriage. In Sūrah 33:59 Mohammed's wives, daughters, and all the womenfolk of the believers are to let down their mantles over them so that they

[45] Stern, *op. cit.*, pp. 62, 69, 70, 174.

would be recognized and not be insulted.[46] These regulations in all probability preceded the "Verse of the Curtain," if only by a short time, since in their scope they cover all Moslem women and in their restrictions are less severe than the institution of the *ḥijāb*, or seclusion. These generally lax moral conditions, calling for such ordinances, no doubt exerted their influence in the direction of seclusion, though they do not seem to have been the only or the direct cause of it. Since this institution when first adopted in Islam affected the wives of Mohammed only, one must look to Mohammed and his wives for direct and specific factors in its adoption.

There has been an unhappy tendency among some Western biographers of Mohammed to credit this particular institution largely, if not indeed solely, to his pronounced and avowed weakness for the fair sex. That this weakness played an important part is not to be denied; that it played the sole or even the major part is to be questioned. Sexual desire and jealousy, family honor and social prestige, as well as religious and political ambitions were all at work to bring about this and other regulations for the prophet's wives. We have already mentioned the episode at Zainab's wedding, which though widely accepted is not the only one of the first type of factors just listed. There is, for instance, a tradition which asserts that the *ḥijāb* was instituted because the hands of some of Mohammed's wives touched those of some of the men

[46] Cf. Ibn Saʿd, VIII, 136 f.

at a common meal, and variants add further that it was the hand of Aishah that touched that of ᶜUmar.[47] This particular story may well be a fabrication, but with such reputed beauties as Aishah,[48] Umm Salamah, and Zainab in his harem, all proud, gay, and free in a loose and frivolous society, Mohammed might well be jealous of seemingly trivial familiarities.

Traditions associating the institution of seclusion with family honor and social prestige refer to insults offered Mohammed's wives by the *munāfiqūn*, or "hypocrites," who, on being taken to task, excused themselves by saying they had mistaken Mohammed's women for slaves.[49] Sawdah, who was a large and heavy woman, was recognized at a distance and even at night by ᶜUmar, who urged Mohammed thereafter to seclude his women.[50] This would seem to indicate that ᶜUmar feared that others, perhaps again the *munāfiqūn*, recognizing her, might insult or molest her. Or it may mean nothing more than that the stern ᶜUmar, not far removed from his socially humble origins, felt the urge for setting the family of the prophet, who was also his son-in-law, apart from

47 *Ibid.*, p. 126; Baiḍāwī, II, 133.

48 There seems to be no record of a detailed physical description of Aishah or of any of her "sisters." The traditions, taking final form at a time when seclusion had become the rule for the court and upper classes, may be keeping discreet silence on the subject, out of respect to the harem of the prophet. Aishah's young niece and namesake is said to have resembled her distinguished aunt. A detailed description of the younger Aishah is found in *Aghānī*, X, 55 f. However, one may not draw specific points of resemblances from so general a comparison of the two Aishahs.

49 Ibn Saᶜd, VIII, 136 f.

50 Ibn Ḥanbal, VI, 223 and 271.

the common crowd. Other traditions state definitely that ᶜUmar urged Mohammed to seclude his wives, since Mohammed's success brought to the mosque an ever increasing stream of visitors of all sorts.[51] Aishah's house, it is to be remembered, opened onto the court of the mosque,[52] as did probably some of the rest of the adjoining row of apartments where her "sisters" were housed. Seclusion would definitely call for servants to run errands for the mistress; Mohammed's financial position was evidently by now, the fifth year of the *Hijrah,* equal to the situation. Furthermore, a large retinue of servants is one way of enhancing one's social prestige. Many of these servants of both sexes figure later as traditionists.

As the years progressed, crowned with more and more success, both political and economic, Mohammed the prophet took on more and more the function of a king. As prophet-king it was not surprising that he, urged by followers of the type of ᶜUmar, adopted some measure of personal and family exclusiveness in the rough-and-tumble democracy of his day. Closer contacts with and knowledge of the conditions prevailing among the upper classes of some of the surrounding peoples, to whom seclusion and some form of veiling was long known,[53] may also have had its

[51] Bukhārī, III, 312; Nawawī, p. 453; Baiḍāwī, II, 133 f.

[52] Ibn Saᶜd, VIII, 119.

[53] Cf. Caroline Morris Galt, "Veiled Ladies," *American Journal of Archaeology*, XXXV (1931), 373–93; Elizabeth Mary MacDonald, *The Position of Women as Reflected in Semitic Codes of Law* (Toronto, 1931); Stern, *op. cit.*, pp. 109 f.

influence in leading Mohammed to adopt and adapt similar practices for his wives and so raise them to a distinct and superior rank in the now comparatively prosperous politico-religious community. It was for these multiple reasons that Mohammed's wives found themselves, on the one hand, deprived of personal liberty and, on the other hand, raised to a position of honor and dignity. Thus was laid the foundation stone of what was to prove in time one of the most stubborn and retrogressive institutions in Islam—the segregation of the women behind curtain and veil.

Did Mohammed's wives, Aishah included, raise no serious objections to the curtailment of their liberty? The traditions, as far as is known, record no case of rebellion on this score. The aging Sawdah could hardly be expected to protest. Zainab, so closely associated with the institution of the *ḥijāb*, was not likely to question it. The stormy-tempered Ḥafṣah surely feared her stormier father, ʿUmar, who urged and backed Mohammed's action. The proud Umm Salamah may well have resented the new move, but in that case she most probably found herself isolated, for she could hardly expect effective help from the latest addition to the harem, Juwairīyah bint al-Ḥārith, whose wedding to Mohammed seems to have taken place shortly after that of Zainab. That leaves Aishah, whose temperament, we know, was not any less worldly and aggressive than that generally credited to the women of her tribe of Taim.[54] Did she ac-

[54] Abū al-Faraj al-Iṣbahānī, *Kitāb al-Aghānī* (20 vols.; Cairo, 1285/1868), X, 54; cf. Lammens, *op. cit.*, pp. 122 f. and 127.

tually surrender without protest the personal liberty so greatly cherished by the Arab woman of her generation?

Fate and circumstances seem to have conspired against the beloved of Mohammed, for it was just about this time that Aishah was subjected to the severest trial of her young life. The episode, popularly referred to as "the affair of the slander,"[55] took place on the way back to Medina from the expedition against the Banū al-Muṣṭaliq, the very expedition in which Juwairīyah was taken captive. The affair brewed for weeks unsuspected by Aishah and finally developed into a public and scandalous attack on that young woman's virtue. This surely was no time to think of the inconvenience and limitation imposed by seclusion and certainly not the time to protest it. It took a special revelation from heaven to establish Aishah's innocence and restore her to her favored position in Mohammed's harem. The episode passed, but it most probably helped to convince Mohammed and others of the wisdom, under the circumstances, of the practice of seclusion.

However, the seclusion was not so extensive or rigid as one might, at first, be led to think. The women could receive all men within the prohibited degree of marriage.[56] This included the close male blood relatives of father, brothers, uncles, and nephews and close relatives by marriage, such as father-

[55] See below, pp. 29–38.

[56] Ibn Saʿd, VIII, 127 f.; cf. also Qurʾān, Sūrah 4:22 f.; Bukhārī, III, 419 ff.

in-law, stepsons, sisters' and aunts' husbands, since no man was allowed to have two sisters or a niece and her aunt to wife at one and the same time. They could also receive foster-relatives within the prohibited degree of marriage; this included foster fathers, sons, brothers, uncles, and nephews. Since the custom of fosterage was widespread among the Arabs, a woman was likely to have many a male foster-relative. There were two other categories of men from whom Mohammed's wives needed not to exclude themselves. The first included their male slaves unless and until they were liberated. The second covered such men as had no need of women, by which was meant, presumably, eunuchs, since monks and ascetics were frowned on by Mohammed.

Again, Mohammed himself was not, at first at least, a stickler for the strict observation of these relationships. Foster-relationships offered opportunities to follow the letter but not the spirit of its supposed limitations. When Aishah pointed out to Mohammed that it was the wife of a foster-uncle and not the uncle himself who nursed her, Mohammed ignored the point.[57] On another occasion when a secluded woman wished to receive someone not within the above classes, Mohammed simplified matters by suggesting that she give the man some of her milk and so make of him a foster-son. When the woman protested that the man was full grown, Mohammed answered that he was aware of the fact.[58] Whether Mohammed

[57] Ibn Ḥanbal, VI, 33 and 194.

[58] *Ibid.*, pp. 39 and 356.

meant this as a precedent is difficult to say, but Aishah seems to have so considered it,[59] and later herself took advantage of it by creating artificial foster-relationship, through having her sisters or nieces give of their milk to such men as she wished to admit to her presence.[60] But whichever way one may look at the institution of the *ḥijāb*, the consequent seclusion was bound to curtail liberty of action and movement and to confine the women more or less to their limited apartments.

An episode infinitely more trying to the youthful Aishah than the introduction of the *ḥijāb* and the marriage of Mohammed to Zainab and Juwairīyah was the "affair of the slander." It, as already indicated, developed into a scandalous attack on her wifely virtue and faithfulness. The incident, apart from its harem implications, reflected the then current political party trends in Medina at the same time that it served as one of several major motive forces behind Aishah's political intrigues and party support in the succeeding decades. Not all the citizens of Medina were fullheartedly in support of Mohammed. There were those, referred to as the *munāfiqūn*, or the "hypocrites," who resented the privilege and prestige accorded the *muhājirūn*, or "refugees," from Mecca. Foremost among the hypocrites was the Khazrajite ᶜAbd Allah ibn Ubayy, who coveted Mohammed's position of leadership for himself.

[59] *Ibid.*, p. 174; Ibn Saᶜd, VIII, 198.

[60] Ibn Ḥanbal, VI, 271 and 312; cf. Ibn Saᶜd, VIII, 198, 339.

During the course of the expedition against the Banū al-Muṣṭaliq an unfortunate quarrel between some of the men of Medina and some of the refugees was readily seized upon by ᶜAbd Allah, who was on the lookout for incidents that might serve his cause. "If you fatten your dog, he will eat you," he said. "We took these people in and now they are insulting us. They wish to be the masters in our very houses, but, by Allah! when we get back to Medina, we shall see whether the noblest are expelled by the vilest."

These were indeed bold if not traitorous words. ᶜUmar ibn al-Khaṭṭāb was for putting ᶜAbd Allah to death for uttering them, but not so the cooler-headed and more farsighted Mohammed, who answered, "O ᶜUmar! What would men think of a prophet who killed his own followers?" By accepting ᶜAbd Allah's excuses and by giving the order for an immediate march, Mohammed forestalled further trouble on that occasion.[61] But before Medina was reached, fate placed in ᶜAbd Allah's hand an unexpected and powerful weapon—the "affair of the slander."[62]

Aishah and Umm Salamah had accompanied Mohammed on this expedition. On the last day of the return journey orders were given to break camp in the dark and early hours of the morning. Aishah left the crowd and walked out some distance to satisfy a natural need. On her return she missed a necklace of

[61] Ibn Hishām, pp. 725 f.

[62] *Ibid.*, pp. 731–40; Ṭabarī, I, 1517–28; Bukhārī, III, 103–10, 292–301; Ibn Ḥanbal, VI, 59–61, 194–97; cf. Buhl, *Das Leben Muhammeds*, trans. Schaeder (Leipzig, 1930), pp. 281–84.

Yamanite agates that she had been wearing. She retraced her steps in search of it and eventually found it. Returning to the camp, she found the grounds deserted. To her cry for help there came no answer. For the men, assuming Aishah to be in her litter, had placed it on her camel and led it away. They thought nothing of the lightness of the load, for Aishah was a light and slender girl. There was nothing for her now to do but sit and wait in the hopes that her absence would be soon discovered and a search party sent back for her. Waiting there alone, in the still hours of the morning, she soon fell asleep. She awoke to find an embarrassed young man, Ṣafwān ibn al-Muᶜaṭṭal, and his lone camel by her side. Gallantly the young man helped her to mount his camel and silently he led her on the way to Medina. Her absence was not discovered until Mohammed and his party had reached Medina late that afternoon. But presently Ṣafwān arrived leading his camel bearing the missing Aishah.

Mohammed seems to have dismissed the matter there, but not so some of the "faithful" and certainly not the "hypocrites." Here, then, was something ᶜAbd Allah ibn Ubayy could use to discredit Mohammed's cause by bringing disgrace on his family. He, therefore, set out deliberately to aggravate the matter, pointing out, according to some, that, Ṣafwān being young and handsome, it was no wonder that Aishah preferred him to Mohammed. At any rate, he lent a willing ear to the malicious gossip and helped to spread it among the entire community. In this he was aided and abetted by many, among them Zainab's sister, Ḥamnah bint Jaḥsh, who thought to do Zainab some service by helping to pull Aishah down from her high position of favorite. She whispered that other and earlier meetings had taken place between Aishah and Ṣafwān,[63] whom Aishah knew from the days before the seclusion. Even Ḥassān ibn Thābit, Mohammed's court poet, composed some insinuating verses on the matter.[64]

As the days ran into weeks the scandal assumed alarming proportions, yet none dared mention it to Aishah. She, however, had sensed a definite coolness toward her on the part of Mohammed. Something like a month passed before one of the women told her of the scandal that had become the talk of the town. Sick at heart, if not also in body, the young wife asked Mohammed's permission to go to her parents. Umm Rūmān, already aware of the evil rumor, sought to comfort her distressed daughter. "Take comfort, my child," she said gently, "few are the young and beautiful women, more beloved than their rivals, who are not the victims of some scandal." But Aishah would not be consoled. Her sobs brought Abū Bakr to the scene, and, for once, he seemed unequal to the occasion. On their advice Aishah returned to her home in the harem.[65]

[63] *EI*, I, 216; Dermenghem, *Life of Mahomet*, trans. Arabella Yorke (London, 1930), p. 279.

[64] Ibn Hishām, p. 734; Ṭabarī, I, 1522; Bukhārī, III, 105, 300; Ibn Ḥanbal, VI, 60.

[65] Ibn Hishām, p. 733; Ṭabarī, I, 1521 f.

By this time Mohammed himself was no doubt thoroughly alarmed at the magnitude of the scandal and the political significance it could assume. He was, furthermore, probably distracted by his own mixed feelings of tender love for Aishah and taunting doubts of her virtue. Perhaps even more distressing than these was the fact that his revelations had ceased.[66] He decided, therefore, to take a hand in the matter. He could not very well take counsel with Abū Bakr in this affair; and for some reason he overlooked ᶜUmar, perhaps because he remembered ᶜUmar's general severity with the women. He turned instead to Usāmah, the son of his adopted son Zaid ibn Ḥārithah, and ᶜAlī ibn Abī Ṭālib. Usāmah had nothing but good to say of Aishah. ᶜAlī, on the other hand, expressed himself thus: "O Messenger of Allah, Allah has placed no narrow limits on you. Many are the women like her. Examine her maid for the truth of the matter." The maid, a Negress named Barīrah, was accordingly questioned, but she too could associate no such evil with Aishah and dwelt instead on her childish pranks and thoughtless youth. When Mohammed asked Aishah's newest and closest rival, Zainab, what she knew, had heard, or seen of the matter, she swore by Allah that, from what she herself had seen and heard, she knew nothing but good—an answer that won her Aishah's lasting gratitude.[67]

[66] Bukhārī, III, 106, 294 f.; Ibn Ḥanbal, VI, 196.

[67] Ibn Hishām, pp. 734 f.; Ṭabarī, I, 1523; Bukhārī, III, 106, 108, 297; Ibn Ḥanbal, VI, 60, 196 f.; cf. Ibn Manẓūr, *Lisān al-ᶜArab* (20 vols.; Cairo, 1300–1308/1882–91), XVIII, 217.

Encouraged by his investigation so far, Mohammed next took up the matter in public. Standing in the pulpit of the mosque, he addressed the assembled crowd: "O Moslems, who will clear me of all blame if I requite a man who molests my family? For, by Allah, I know naught but good of my family. . . . ."

Either Usaid ibn Ḥuḍair or Saᶜd ibn Muᶜādh, both of the tribe of Aws, rose to the occasion. "I will clear you of all blame," he declared. "If the man is an Awsite, I will strike his head off; and if he is of our brothers the Khazraj, then give your orders regarding him and we shall carry them out."

This brought Saᶜd ibn ᶜUbādah, the chief of the Khazraj, to his feet in hot protest, since he and everyone else knew that the man Mohammed had in mind was the Khazrajite ᶜAbd Allah ibn Ubayy. For his trouble Saᶜd ibn ᶜUbādah was now accused of being a "hypocrite" and a protector of the hypocrites. Accusation and counteraccusation threatened to lead to a free-for-all fight between the Aws and the Khazraj. But Mohammed, keeping cool, succeeded in quieting and pacifying the crowd.[68]

Aishah's tears, in the meantime, continued to flow, and her eyes refused to close in sleep. Next morning her parents visited her, as did also a sympathetic woman of Medina. Presently Mohammed entered, solemnly greeted the group, and, for the first time in about a month, took a seat in Aishah's house.

[68] Ibn Hishām, pp. 733 f.; Ṭabarī, I, 1522 f.; Bukhārī, III, 106 f., 295; Ibn Ḥanbal, VI, 196.

"O Aishah," he pleaded, "if you are innocent, Allah will absolve you. But if you are guilty, ask forgiveness of Allah and repent, for Allah pardons those of his servants who confess and repent."

She made no answer, expecting her parents to rise to her defense; but they too held their peace. Struggling to keep her tears in check, she turned first to her father and then to her mother, asking that they give answer to Mohammed, but only to be told by each in turn, "I know not what answer to make to the Messenger of Allah!" So unequal were they to the occasion, and so little did they seem to have of faith in or knowledge of the true character of their young daughter. Stung by their attitude and sustained by her innocence, she rose in her own defense, speaking with tearful yet calm determination and with admirable pride:

> I see that you have listened to this talk about me until it has taken hold of you and you now believe in it. If I say I am innocent—and Allah most high knows that I am—you will not believe me. But if I confess to anything—and Allah most high knows that I am innocent—you will surely believe me. There remains nothing for me to do but say, with Joseph's father, "Patience is becoming, and Allah's help is to be implored."[69]

Her speech delivered, she retired to her bed, fully expecting Allah to take a hand in establishing her innocence.[70] Her deliverance was near at hand, for presently Mohammed began to show some of the

[69] Sūrah 12:18.

[70] Ibn Hishām, p. 735; Ṭabarī, I, 1523 f.; Bukhārī, III, 107 f., 295 f.; Ibn Ḥanbal, VI, 60, 196 f.

physical symptoms generally accompanying his revelations. Coming out of his spell with a smiling face, his first words were for the patient and courageous young wife.

"Good tidings, O Aishah," he called out to her. "Allah most high has exonerated you."

"Rise and come to Mohammed," urged her parents.

"I shall neither come to him nor thank him. Nor will I thank the both of you who listened to the slander and did not deny it. I shall rise," she concluded, "to give thanks to Allah alone."[71]

Mohammed went out to the people and gave utterance to his revelations which are to be found in Sūrah 24 of the Qur'ān and which still form the Islamic law of adultery. The verses bearing directly on the affair of the slander against Aishah read as follows:

> Verily those who produced the lie are a small faction amongst you; do not consider it evil for you, rather is it good for you; every man of them will bear the guilt he has earned for himself, and for him amongst them who was responsible for the bulk of it is (in store) punishment mighty.
>
> Why, when ye heard it, did not the believing men and believing women form in their minds a good opinion and say: "This is a lie manifest"?
>
> Why have they not brought four witnesses regarding it? Seeing then that they have not brought the witnesses, they are in Allah's eyes the speakers of falsehood.
>
> Had it not been for the bounty and mercy of Allah towards you in this world and the Hereafter there would have affected you in the matter of your unguarded talk punishment mighty.
>
> When ye were taking it from each others' tongues and saying

[71] Ibn Ḥanbal, VI, 60, 197; Bukhārī, III, 108, 296.

with your mouths things of which ye had no knowledge, and thinking it a light matter, while in Allah's eyes it was mighty. Why, when ye heard it, did ye not say: "It is not for us to talk about this; glory be to Thee! this is slander mighty"?

Allah admonisheth you never to do the like again, if ye be believers.[72]

ᶜAbd Allah ibn Ubayy's position in Medina was such that, though he was known to have been the prime mover in the matter of the slander, he yet escaped with no worse punishment than the threats in the above verses. Ḥamnah bint Jaḥsh, Ḥassān ibn Thābit, and a lesser scandalmonger, Misṭaḥ ibn Uthāthah, were flogged in public.[73] Ṣafwān avenged himself on Ḥassān by striking him with his sword. Mohammed reprimanded both men and then soothed Ḥassān's hurt and pride by a generous gift. The poet, in his turn, composed new verses in praise of Aishah, who soon came to forgive him and who in later years refused to hear evil spoken of the then blind poet, saying that he had given his talents in the service of Allah and his prophet.[74] Neither did she forget the good words of Zainab bint Jaḥsh,[75] and for Usāmah ibn Zaid, who had defended her, she developed a lasting friendship.[76] But for ᶜAlī she harbored a strong

[72] Sūrah 24:11–16; for the translation cf. Richard Bell, *Qurʾān* (2 vols.; Edinburgh, 1937–39), I, 336 f.

[73] Ibn Hishām, p. 736, 740; Ṭabarī, I, 1525.

[74] Ibn Hishām, pp. 737–39; Ṭabarī, I, 1526–28; Bukhārī, III, 105, 110, 298; *Aghānī*, IV, 14 f.; cf. Hirschfeld, *The Dīwān of Ḥassān ibn Thābit* (London, 1910), pp. 6, 50, 62.

[75] Cf. above, p. 33 and below, p. 99.

[76] Ibn Ḥanbal, VI, 156 f.

dislike if not indeed enmity. This was to find expression in her repeated attempts to thwart ᶜAlī's personal and political ambitions in the course of the following decades.

Thanks to Allah's intervention, Mohammed's affection, and her own proud and fearless spirit, Aishah resumed her position as Mohammed's favorite and the first lady of his harem—a position that was to grow all the more secure as Mohammed's few remaining years were drawing to their end. None of her harem "sisters" was able to challenge it. Most of them had occasion to resent it, but only the more aggressive among the harem opposition party had the courage openly to protest it.

Mohammed's harem in the meantime continued to increase. In the two-year period following his marriage to Zainab and Juwairīyah, from the spring of 627 to that of 629, five new inmates joined the six "sisters" of his household. The first was a beautiful young Jewess, Raiḥānah bint Zaid, of the Banū Naḍīr. She had married into the tribe of the Banū Quraiẓah and had lost her husband and other male relatives in the wholesale massacre of the latter tribe. Tradition is undecided as to her proper status in the harem. According to some, she was a full-fledged wife holding the same rank as the rest; but, according to others, she preferred to remain a slave concubine, a status in which she could retain her old faith and escape the limitations of seclusion. One hears little about her that is tangible except that she died about a year before Mohammed.[77] Another Jewess to join Mohammed's harem in this period was Ṣafīyah bint Ḥuayy, the beautiful seventeen-year-old widow of Kinānah, chief of the Jews of Khaibar, who lost his life on the unhappy occasion of the Moslem reduction of that town. Unlike Raiḥānah, Ṣafīyah seems to have been a fickle opportunist who readily accepted Islam and flattered its prophet.[78] The third girl to catch Mohammed's fancy was the young and curly-headed slave girl, Mary the Copt. She and her sister were, strangely enough, the gift of the Christian governor of Egypt sent to Mohammed in the Year 7 of the *Hijrah*. Her status was that of a concubine. She seems to have been housed at first close by, where Mohammed visited her frequently by day and night. The jealous harem, however, soon made things unpleasant for her, and she was moved to a house in Upper Medina, where her son Ibrāhīm was born in the Year 8 and where she herself died some five years after Mohammed.[79]

It was undoubtedly the youthful charm and beauty of these three that won the acquisitive heart of Mohammed. But it was political policy that dictated his other two marriages of this same period. The first was with Ramlah, daughter of Abū Sufyān, the leader of

[77] Ibn Saᶜd, VIII, 92–94 and 159; *Iṣābah*, IV, 591 f.; Muir, *Life of Mohammed*, ed. Weir (Edinburgh, 1923), pp. 318 f.

[78] Ibn Saᶜd, VIII, 85–92; *Iṣābah*, IV, 666–69; cf. Muir, *op. cit.*, pp. 377 f.

[79] Ibn Saᶜd, VIII, 153; *Iṣābah*, IV, 779 f.; cf. Muir, *op. cit.*, pp. 371 and 425 f.

the Meccan opposition. She had early accepted Islam in defiance of her father and had migrated to Abyssinia with her husband, who died there. Tradition would have us believe that it was the Abyssinian Negus himself who arranged her marriage to Mohammed, soon after the Treaty of Ḥudaibīyah. She was at that time about thirty-five years of age, so that Mohammed's marriage to her was in all probability either a bid for a more friendly relationship with her father or a subtle defiant gesture reflecting Mohammed's recent successes and consolidation of influence and power.[80] Abū Sufyān's reaction to the marriage was that "is a camel stallion not to be tapped on (that is, led by) the nose!"[81] The next and last wife to join the harem was Maimūnah bint al-Ḥārith, whose wedding is generally believed to have taken place in Shawwāl of the Year 7 of the *Hijrah* (March–April, A.D. 629). She was a young and comely widow of twenty-six who had intrusted her personal affairs to her brother-in-law, the influential ᶜAbbās, uncle of Mohammed. She was, furthermore, the aunt of Khālid ibn al-Walīd, the recently converted general and future "Sword of Allah."[82]

This rapid growth of Mohammed's harem—the addition within about two short years of seven inmates beginning with Zainab bint Jaḥsh—increased in proportion the jealousies of the numerous rivals

[80] Ibn Saᶜd, VIII, 68–71; *Iṣābah,* IV, 584–87; cf. Muir, *op. cit.,* p. 372.

[81] Ibn Saᶜd, VIII, 70.

[82] Ibn Saᶜd, VIII, 94–100; Nawawī, pp. 224 f.; *Iṣābah,* I, 107.

both old and new. Seclusion, by narrowing the interests of the women, gave an added importance to the affairs of the harem. To keep the peace, Mohammed made an effort at an impartial routine. He allotted each full-fledged wife her day or turn and so rotated among them all. Since he could not take all of them on his raids or pilgrimages, he cast lots among them to determine the one or more who were to accompany him. When it came to worldly goods, he strove not to favor one above the other. But when it came to the affairs of the heart, even he realized that there impartiality was a vain hope; and, when hard pressed, he openly acknowledged, as will be seen presently, that Aishah was his best beloved. Only an incurable optimist could hope for continual peace in the harem under such circumstances. And peace Mohammed did not always have.

Mohammed's harem, as already stated, was divided into two parties, reflecting social and political status and ambitions.[83] The group in power dominated by Aishah included from the start the quick-tempered Ḥafṣah and the stout and aging Sawdah. From these she had little to fear, since they lacked the personal charm with which to bid successfully for the affections of Mohammed. Sawdah, realizing how matters stood between her and Mohammed, who, she feared, was about to divorce her, eventually made a virtue of necessity and yielded her "turn" or "day" to Aishah. She hoped thereby to avert the divorce

[83] See above, pp. 15 f.

and so still retain her position of rank in the harem, so as to share with the rest of Mohammed's wives their expected reward in heaven.[84] To this group of three was added later the young Jewess Ṣafīyah. There is a very human account of the curiosity of several of Mohammed's wives about the new rival on her arrival at Medina with Mohammed after the expedition against Khaibar. Among the curious women of Medina who came out to see the prophet's new wife, who was reputed to be very beautiful, were Aishah and Ḥafṣah and also Zainab and Juwairīyah.

"I fear," said Zainab to her companion, "this woman will get ahead of us with Mohammed."

"Nay," answered Juwairīyah; "she is not the kind that finds much favor with husbands."

Mohammed had recognized Aishah among the group. When she left, he followed her to ask her opinion of her latest rival.

"She is but a Jewess," was Aishah's short answer.

"Say not so, O Aishah, for she has become a good Moslem," came Mohammed's gentle rebuke.

But Aishah and Ḥafṣah could not apparently refrain from taunting the newcomer with her racial origin. It was Mohammed himself who, in the end, coached her to retort: "How can you be above me when Aaron is my father, Moses is my uncle, and Mohammed is my husband!"[85] This worked effectively when Ḥafṣah, jealous because Mohammed pre-

[84] Ibn Saᶜd, VIII, 31 f., 121 f.; Ibn Ḥanbal, VI, 68, 76 f.

[85] Ibn Saᶜd, VIII, 80 f.; *Iṣābah*, IV, 668.

ferred Ṣafīyah's company to hers, once more taunted her with being a Jewess.[86] For some little time at least Ṣafīyah must have continued to find favor with Mohammed, since both Umm Salamah and Zainab were jealous of her. The latter incurred Mohammed's displeasure for several months for refusing the gift of a camel to the Jewess in an emergency on one of the pilgrimages.[87] It was in connection with this episode that Ṣafīyah, fearing she had displeased Mohammed, asked Aishah to help reinstate her in his favor. In return she yielded her "turn" to Aishah for that day. Aishah, wearing her gay saffron-colored and perfumed outer garment, went over to Mohammed's tent and sat by his side.

"What is it you wish, O Aishah?" he asked. "It is not your turn today."

"That is the gift of Allah given to whom he pleases," she answered confidently and then told her story, which had the desired effect of reconciling him to Ṣafīyah.[88] In the long run, however, Juwairīyah's estimate of Ṣafīyah's charms seems to have been justified, for in his later days Mohammed lost interest in her as he seems to have done in all of his wives excepting Aishah, Umm Salamah, and Zainab.[89]

Aishah seems to have had little or no difficulty in

[86] *Iṣābah*, IV, 769 f.

[87] Ibn Saᶜd, VIII, 67; Ibn Ḥanbal, VI, 131 f., 261, 337 f.

[88] Ibn Ḥanbal, VI, 145, 337 f.

[89] Ibn Saᶜd, VIII, 141 f.; Yaᶜqūbī, *Tārīkh* ("Historiae"), ed. Houtsma (2 vols.; Lugduni Batavorum, 1883), II, 93, adds Ḥafṣah.

securing the co-operation of any one of the three in her group—Ḥafṣah, Sawdah, and Ṣafīyah—for any plot, harmless or otherwise, either against a member of the group itself[90] or against a rival in the harem opposition party. There is, for instance, the well-known episode of Mohammed and the honey. In this, according to some accounts, Aishah, Sawdah, and Ṣafīyah ganged up against Ḥafṣah;[91] but, according to others, it was Aishah and Ḥafṣah who plotted against either Zainab[92] or Umm Salamah.[93] The essentials of the playful plot in all three versions are so similar that the different details in the various accounts must be taken as supplementary. Furthermore, since Ḥafṣah was never a favorite with Mohammed, and since Zainab and Umm Salamah were a close second to Aishah,[94] the plot was in all probability directed against one of them and not against Ḥafṣah. Mohammed seems to have been in the habit of stopping for a short visit with each of his wives before he retired to the apartment of the one whose "turn" it was for the night. One day he tarried unusually long at the house of either Zainab or Umm Salamah, enjoying a treat of honey, of which delicacy he was very fond. Aishah took jealous note and coached her group to ask him, as he came to them on

[90] Cf. above, pp. 11 f.

[91] Ibn Saʿd, VIII, 59; Ibn Ḥanbal, VI, 59; Bukhārī, III, 462 f.

[92] Ibn Saʿd, VIII, 76; Ibn Ḥanbal, VI, 221; Bukhārī, III, 358, 462, and IV, 273 f.; Nasāʾī, *Sunan* (Cairo, 1312/1894), I, 141 f.

[93] Ibn Saʿd, VIII, 122 f.

[94] *Ibid.*, pp. 81 and 73.

that day's rounds, if he had eaten *maghāfīr*, the strong-smelling gum of the *ʿurfuṭ* tree. They followed up his expected "No" with, "Why, then, have you so strong a breath?"

"Zainab (or Umm Salamah) gave me some honey to drink."

"The bees that made that honey must have devoured the *ʿurfuṭ*," they persisted.

Mohammed, who was very sensitive about personal odors, refused honey the next time it was offered to him. Sawdah, fearing they had carried the joke too far, remarked that they were depriving Mohammed of his favorite honey. But Aishah, apparently concerned only about the disclosure of her part in the plot, ordered the considerate Sawdah to keep quiet.[95]

More lively and even stormy scenes involved Aishah and the second group of wives in Mohammed's harem. Despite Mohammed's genuine effort to deal fairly and impartially with all his wives, all the Moslem community knew that Aishah was his favorite. Members of the community, thinking to please Mohammed, picked on Aishah's "day" as the best time to send any gift they had for him. Mohammed, whenever possible, distributed these gifts, which were frequently household provisions, among his harem.[96] Still the other wives, particularly those in Umm Salamah's group, resented the pointed discrimination on the part of the gift-making public. They commis-

[95] Cf. above, p. 44, n. 91. [96] Cf. below, pp. 49 f.

sioned Umm Salamah to appeal to Mohammed to put a stop to this practice by asking the Moslems to send their gifts to the different apartments. She broached the subject to him, but he received it in silence. Her group urged her to try again and again until she did get an answer. She showed no reluctance to comply with their request, but the only answer she finally received was, "Trouble me not about Aishah. She is the only woman in whose company I receive any revelations."

"Allah forgive me for troubling you," answered the subdued Umm Salamah.[97]

The rest of her group, however, were not content to let it go at that. They sent his daughter Fāṭimah to plead their cause. Having first forced from the reluctant Fāṭimah that Zainab was responsible for the new move, Mohammed completely floored his daughter by asking, "Dear little daughter, do you not love whom I love?"

"Yes, surely," was all she could think of to say. And nothing the discontented wives could say would induce her to try again. Zainab now decided to take up the matter in person. Disregarding Aishah's presence, she loudly protested the partiality shown the favorite. Mohammed and Aishah watched each other for a reaction. Meanwhile, Zainab, perhaps sensing failure, lost control of herself and heaped abuse and insult on Aishah. "Defend yourself," came Mohammed's encouragement to Aishah. Defend herself she

[97] Bukhārī, II, 132 f.; Ibn Ḥanbal, VI, 293; Ibn Saʿd, VIII, 117.

did with a vengeance and soon had the discomfited Zainab reduced to silence. Mohammed, watching the performance, closed the incident with this admiring pronouncement on his victorious favorite: "She is indeed the daughter of her father!"[98]

Still another incident is recorded in which Aishah came out the victor in a vituperative battle with either Zainab or Umm Salamah, most probably the latter; for it was she and not Zainab who generally sought to identify herself with the family of Fāṭimah and ᶜAlī,[99] both of whom became involved in this affair. Outraged at Mohammed's display of affection for Aishah in her presence, the proud Makhzūmite, who had in the days of her courtship warned Mohammed of her jealousy, exclaimed indignantly, "I see that the rest of us are as nothing in your presence." She proceeded to vent the rest of her wrath on Aishah, abusing her roundly. Mohammed tried to calm her but failed. He, therefore, ordered his favorite to answer her in kind, and in this she did not disappoint him. The disgruntled Umm Salamah betook herself to Fāṭimah and ᶜAlī, between both of whom and Aishah not much love was lost. She told them not only of the abuse she had received but of some that Aishah had apparently heaped on them also. ᶜAlī, so the story goes, sent Fāṭimah to protest to her father.

[98] See preceding note and Ibn Ḥanbal, VI, 88, 93, 150 f.; Ibn Saᶜd, VIII, 123 f.

[99] Ibn Ḥanbal, VI, 292, 298, 304.

"By the Lord of the Kaᶜbah," swore Mohammed, "Aishah is your father's best beloved!" The timid Fāṭimah reported her failure to ᶜAlī, who now went in person to Mohammed.

"Was it not enough for you," he asked, "that Aishah should have insulted us, but you must needs tell Fāṭimah that she is your best beloved?"[100]

Mohammed's answer is not recorded. But shortly after the episode, he had the door between the harem proper and the adjoining apartment of Fāṭimah and ᶜAlī sealed.[101]

It was only in defense of the faithful Khadījah that Mohammed once rebuked Aishah. Growing jealous of his tender memory of the long-departed Khadījah, Aishah referred to her as "that toothless old woman whom Allah had replaced with a better." She drew on herself a quick rebuke from a displeased and agitated Mohammed, who exclaimed, "Nay, indeed, Allah has not replaced her by a better. She believed in me when I was rejected; when they called me a liar, she proclaimed me truthful; when I was poor, she shared with me her wealth; and Allah granted me her children though withholding those of other women."[102]

A more serious situation developed which led Mo-

[100] *Ibid.*, p. 130.

[101] Lammens, *Fātima et les filles de Mahomet* (Rome, 1912), pp. 47 f.

[102] Ibn Ḥanbal, VI, 117 f. and 154; *Iṣābah*, IV, 541 f. For an account of Khadījah's role in the life of Mohammed see Abbott, "Women and the State in Early Islam," *Journal of Near Eastern Studies* (*JNES*), I (1942), 121–23.

hammed to separate himself from all his wives for an entire month, at the end of which he gave them a choice between Allah and his prophet or the world and its pleasures. Major as the crisis was, the traditions give it no specific date and differ widely as to its immediate cause. There is first a group of traditions which indicate that Mohammed's wives plagued him for more worldly goods than were within his reach. An amusing anecdote is related of how one day Mohammed was besieged by his wives, who loudly clamored for clothes. When presently ᶜUmar was announced, they fled so hastily behind the *ḥijāb*, or curtain, that Mohammed could not help laughing at their plight. ᶜUmar took them to task for being more afraid of him than of Mohammed, and they answered from behind the curtain, "You are rougher and harsher than the Messenger of Allah."[103] Did these women, confined to their apartments, seek consciously or unconsciously some sort of tangible compensation for the loss of their liberty in the demand for more worldly goods? At any rate, demands for worldly goods are not incompatible with the phraseology of the "Verse of the Choice."[104]

There is another group of traditions which associate the crisis with the jealous Aishah. One day while in Aishah's house, Mohammed, it seems, had either received a gift or had ordered an animal butchered. He asked Aishah to divide it among his wives, and he

[103] Ibn Saᶜd, VIII, 130 f.; cf. Stern, *op. cit.*, p. 114.

[104] Cf. Ibn Saᶜd, VIII, 129 ff.; Baiḍāwī, II, 127.

sent Zainab her share. Not being satisfied with it, Zainab returned it, whereupon Mohammed asked Aishah to add to it, and he sent it back to her. This, according to some of the versions, was repeated thrice. Aishah, now indignant, remarked to Mohammed, "This contemptuous woman is causing you to lose face!"

"You (women)," answered the angry Mohammed, "are (in truth) more contemptuous of Allah than of me! I shall not visit you for a month."[105]

There is still a third group of traditions which involve Mohammed's conduct with Mary the Copt. According to one version, Ḥafṣah caught Mohammed and Mary in her own apartment, but on Aishah's day.[106] She let Mohammed know that she had seen them, and he begged her not to tell Aishah, promising in return to forego Mary's company thereafter. Ḥafṣah promised but broke her word. She hastened to tell Aishah the good news that Mohammed had forsworn Mary's company, for the entire harem were jealous of the fair and curly-headed Coptic concubine. According to a second version of this episode of Mohammed and Mary, the incident took place on Ḥafṣah's day, making her the chief injured party.[107] In both versions, however, it was Aishah who took Mohammed to task for the indiscreet infringement of

[105] Ibn Saᶜd, VIII, 136 f. I have not seen this story elsewhere.

[106] *Ibid.*, p. 134; Ṭabarī, *Tafsīr* (30 vols.; Cairo, 1321/1903), XXVIII, 91.

[107] Ibn Saᶜd, VIII, 133 f.

the harem rules. Soon the entire harem was up in arms, and Mohammed, exasperated, retired from all his wives.

This episode of Mary the Copt may or may not have been the immediate occasion that precipitated this major harem crisis. But there can be little doubt that it was contributory to it, since Mohammed's wives were not likely to make an issue of an affair that involved Mary and Mohammed *after* a crisis which so humiliated them and which, ending with the "Verse of the Choice," placed more drastic regulations on the entire harem, subduing, in a measure, even such bold leaders as Aishah, Ḥafṣah, and Umm Salamah. Aside from Mary's connection with the crisis, there are other bits of information which tend to place the incident in the Year 7 or after. The crisis took place when a Ghassānid invasion was expected, and this is generally believed to have been comparatively late in the Medinan period, and the cause of Mohammed's expedition to Tabūk in 9/630.[108] Some of the traditions do indeed assign the "Verse of the Choice" to the ninth year of the *Hijrah*.[109] The number of Mohammed's wives at the time of the choice was generally taken for granted to be nine.[110] A list of nine wives would have to include Ṣafīyah; it would also have to include Maimūnah, unless Raiḥānah is to be counted as a full-fledged wife instead of a concubine. The one known list of those of Mohammed's wives who were

[108] Cf. Muir, *op. cit.*, pp. 439 f.

[109] *Iṣābah*, IV, 873.

[110] Ibn Saᶜd, VIII, 145.

given "the choice" does actually include both Ṣafīyah and Maimūnah. A tribal woman with whom Mohammed was contracting a marriage supposedly in the Year 8, elected to leave him at the time of "the choice." Unfortunately, however, both of the preceding traditions can be questioned, the first because it is a singleton tradition[111] and the second because of some uncertainty as to the identity of the woman in question and as to the real motive of her separation from Mohammed.[112]

From the traditions giving ᶜUmar's and others' accounts of Mohammed's withdrawal from his wives,[113] it is apparent that these women did not hesitate to speak their minds in answer to or in argument with Mohammed. It is equally clear that they considered it their right to demand worldly goods from him. Furthermore, these accounts seem to have confused at least two or perhaps even three separate occasions, compounding them into one episode. They contain definite indications that ᶜUmar had been informed on some previous occasion(s) of the conditions prevailing in Mohammed's harem by his own wife in defense of her own similar conduct and that the information had been openly confirmed by his daughter Ḥafṣah. Much displeased and a little alarmed, he gave his daughter some stern advice: "Do not be excessive in

[111] Cf. Stern, *op. cit.*, p. 118.

[112] Ibn Saᶜd, VIII, 138 and 100–102.

[113] *Ibid.*, pp. 129–39; Bukhārī, II, 103–6, III, 359 f., 442–44; Ibn Ḥanbal, I, 33 f.

your demands on Mohammed or contradict and talk back to him, or shun his company; ask me for your needs; and do not be jealous of your (rival) neighbor and companion, Aishah, who is fairer and more beloved of Mohammed than you are."[114]

Either on that or on another similar occasion, ᶜUmar proceeded to see Mohammed. He found him depressed and asked the cause of his troubles. Mohammed answered that his wives had been pestering him for things beyond his ability to provide. ᶜUmar then told of his own experiences with his wife and of the advice he had already given Ḥafṣah, adding that the prophet surely could handle his wives with firmness. Mohammed was somewhat amused, and his good spirits began to return. But ᶜUmar was not content to let matters rest there. He headed for Ḥafṣah's house and on the way met Abū Bakr and told him of his interview with Mohammed. Then each went to caution his daughter not to ask Mohammed for things but to let him, her father, know of her needs. ᶜUmar, either alone or accompanied by Abū Bakr, according to one version, now went the rounds of the harem, admonishing each wife in turn until Umm Salamah undertook to speak up to him.

"O ᶜUmar," she protested, "must you interfere even in the harem affairs? Whom then should we ask for our needs if not the prophet?" Rebuffed in his self-imposed mission, ᶜUmar departed, while Umm Salamah won the admiration and gratitude of the

[114] Ibn Saᶜd, VIII, 131 f.; Bukhārī, III, 442 f.

rest of the "sisterhood," who were too timid to dare cross words with this fiery man.[115] The episode seems to have passed, with the wives still holding their own.

When presently the real crisis actually developed, the news of it was brought to ʿUmar by his *anṣār* "brother," Aws ibn Khawlayy, whose business it was to keep ʿUmar informed of any report or event of importance. To Aws and the crowd around the mosque, the rumor of mass divorce threatened a graver result than an expected Ghassānid invasion. Part of the gravity is to be explained by the effect such a move would have on the relationship between Mohammed and his politically powerful fathers-in-law, Abū Bakr and ʿUmar, and, if Maimūnah was involved, there would also be her nephew, Khālid ibn al-Walīd, to reckon with. ʿUmar hastened to Ḥafṣah, whom he found in tears.

"Did I not warn you against this?" cried this Job's comforter. "Are you divorced?" he demanded impatiently.

"I do not know," she answered, still crying. "He is alone in the loft."[116]

Even Umm Salamah is said to have been reduced to tears now.[117] ʿUmar went next to the mosque, passing through the assembled crowds waiting to know the facts and the final outcome of the matter. When ʿUmar was first announced, Mohammed silently ig-

[115] Ibn Saʿd, VIII, 129 and 137; Bukhārī, III, 359.

[116] Bukhārī, III, 443; *Iṣābah,* IV, 522.

[117] Ibn Saʿd, VIII, 133.

nored the fact. Again he was announced and again ignored. On the third request Mohammed gave permission for him to enter. This time ᶜUmar did not ask what the trouble was but went straight to the point:

"Have you divorced your wives?" he asked.

"No," came the brief answer.

"*Allah Akbar*, God is most great," sang out ᶜUmar in his rich and sonorous voice. The waiting crowds and anxious wives knew that a serious social and political crisis had been averted.[118] ᶜUmar, in all probability seconded by Abū Bakr, who on occasion could be harsh enough to the point of striking Aishah,[119] seized the opportunity once more to ingratiate themselves with Mohammed and to admonish their daughters and the harem in general.[120] Mohammed, in the meantime, remained alone in his loft for the completion of the month. He then resumed his harem rounds, beginning with Aishah, who received him with:

"I but spoke a thoughtless word and you lost your temper with me. Did you not say," she added impudently, "that you would stay away for a month, and here it is only twenty-nine days!"

"This month," Mohammed answered, "has twenty-nine days only."

But Aishah soon found out that the matter was not to be so easily dismissed. Mohammed had a serious

[118] *Ibid.*, pp. 132 f., 136; Bukhārī, III, 445.

[119] Ibn Saᶜd, VIII, 56; cf. also Ibn Ḥanbal, IV, 271 f. and 275.

[120] Ṭabarī, *Tafsīr*, XXVIII, 94; *Iṣābah*, IV, 522.

proposition to make to her and advised her to consult her parents before making her decision. It was then that he repeated to her the "Verse of the Choice":

> O Prophet, say to thy wives: If ye desire the life of this world and its adornment, then come, I shall make a provision for you and send you forth honorably; but if ye desire Allah and his Messenger and the future abode, then Allah has prepared for those of you who do well a mighty reward.[121]

"I need not to consult my parents," she answered without any hesitation. "You know they would never advise me to leave you. I desire Allah and his Messenger." She requested him, however, not to reveal her decision to the rest of his wives when he proposed the same choice to them. Mohammed refused to comply and saw to it that the rest of the harem knew of Aishah's choice. One after another, all followed in the footsteps of the favorite and chose Allah and his Messenger.[122]

This was undoubtedly a good time to introduce new harem regulations, calculated to subdue the inmates. The nature and extent of these are to be found in a group of verses that follow the "Verse of the Choice":

> O wives of the Prophet, whoever of you commits a manifest indecency, for her the punishment will be doubled twice over; for Allah that is easy.
>
> But to whoever of you is obedient to Allah and his Messenger, and acts uprightly, we shall give her reward twice over, and we have prepared for her a noble provision.

[121] Sūrah 33:28–29; Bell, *op. cit.*, II, 413.

[122] Ibn Saᶜd, VIII, 47, 130, 133; Ibn Ḥanbāl, VI, 78, 185, 211 f.

O wives of the Prophet, ye are not like any ordinary woman; if ye are pious, then do not be too complaisant of speech lest he in whose heart is disease grow lustful, but speak in reputable fashion.

Remain in your houses and do not swagger about in the manner of the former paganism. Observe prayer and give alms and obey Allah and his Messenger; Allah simply wishes to take away the pollution from you, O people of the house, and to purify you thoroughly.

And call to mind the signs of Allah and the wisdom which are recited in your houses. . . . .[123]

It is to be noted that, in connection with the harem crisis, Mohammed's wives are referred to generally as his "wives" or his "women" and not as the "Mothers of the Believers." It is highly improbable that they had before then acquired that title and dignity and, as most commentators believe, the consequent prohibition of remarriage even after Mohammed's death. The revelations concerned are to be found in the first and last part of Sūrah 33:6 and 53, respectively:

The Prophet is nearer to the believers than themselves, and his wives are their mothers. . . . .

It is not for you to insult the Messenger of Allah, or ever to marry his wives after him; verily that is grievous in the sight of Allah.

The "Verse of the Choice" means nothing at all if it does not mean that those who "desired the world and its adornment" were free to marry again after being divorced by Mohammed. The title and the prohibition were most probably more closely associated with the harem crisis than with the earlier occasion of

[123] Sūrah 33:30–35; Bell, *op. cit.*, II, 414.

the institution of the *ḥijāb*, or seclusion. With threats and rumors of divorce, there doubtless were some men who had eyes on some of the harem beauties so involved. Or the occasion for these verses may have come even later when Mohammed's advancing age and failing health led some ambitious men, in anticipation of his death, to cast eyes on those of his wives as appealed to them.[124] There are traditions that indicate that Aishah's cousin, Ṭalḥah ibn ᶜUbaid Allah, had such designs on her. This was the same Ṭalḥah who had been among the earliest converts to Islam, ably active in its wars, and highly esteemed by Mohammed, Abū Bakr, and ᶜUmar. It was he who had accompanied Aishah with Abū Bakr's family on their journey from Mecca to Medina. It was again he who, in the preliminaries of the Battle of the Khandaq (5/627), came gallantly to Aishah's rescue when ᶜUmar saw fit to take her severely to task for daring to venture out alone in order to explore the situation herself.[125] Ties of blood, political ambition, and the lovely Aishah's personal charms may well have turned Ṭalḥah's thoughts and eyes toward this beloved wife of Mohammed. Tradition relates that he was heard to say that he would marry Aishah in the event of Mohammed's death, and that when Mohammed heard this he received the revelation prohibiting the remarriage of his wives.[126] It is interesting to note

[124] Cf. Ibn Saᶜd, VIII, 145.

[125] Ibn Ḥanbāl, VI, 141; Ibn Saᶜd, III^{1}, 3; Ṭabarī, I, 1478.

[126] Ibn Saᶜd, VIII, 145.

that Ṭalḥah later married Aishah's younger half-sister, Umm Kulthūm, whose hand Aishah had guardedly refused to ʿUmar, caliph though he was at that time, because of his well-known severity toward the women, his own wives included.[127]

A number of ordinances, some either relieving Mohammed of tiresome harem restrictions or releasing him from some oaths, others regulating and restricting further the women's conduct, and still others threatening them with divorce, belong most probably in this period of the crisis or soon after; though again traditionists and commentators are not agreed as to the specific time or reason for their issuance.[128] These are to be found in Sūrah 66:1–5, which reads as follows:

O Prophet, why doest thou make prohibited what Allah has made allowable for thee, out of desire for the approval of thy wives? Allah is forgiving, compassionate.

Allah hath made legal for you the annulling of your oaths; Allah is your patron, and He is the Knowing, the Wise.

(Recall) when the Prophet made a story secret to one of his wives; then when she announced it and Allah made that appear to him, he made known part of it and avoided part; then when he told it to her, she said: "Who gave thee this information?" He replied: "It was told me by the Knowing, the Well-informed."

If ye two repent towards Allah, then your hearts are well inclined, but if ye back each other up against him, then Allah is his patron, and Gabriel, and the upright among the Believers; and beyond that the angels are backing (for him).

It is possible that if he divorce you, his Lord will give him in exchange wives better than you, Moslems, believers, devout,

[127] Ibn Saʿd, III¹, 152; cf. below, p. 88.

[128] Cf., e.g., Ibn Saʿd, VIII, 129–39; Baiḍāwī, II, 340 f.

repentant, given to worship and fasting, both women who have been already married and virgins.[129]

Still another group of verses concerning Mohammed's wives and providing this time for special marriage privileges for the prophet belong most probably to a somewhat later period. They are to be found in Sūrah 33:49–52 and read as follows:

O Prophet, We have made allowable for thee thy wives to whom thou hast given their hires, those whom thou hast taken into thy possession from the spoil which Allah has given thee as property, the daughters of thy uncles or thy aunts either on the father's or the mother's side who have emigrated with thee, and any believing woman, if she offer herself to the Prophet, and the Prophet wish to take her in marriage; (this is) special for thee and does not apply to the believers—

We know what We have laid upon them as a duty in the matter of their wives, and those whom they have taken into their possession—in order that there may be no blame upon thee; Allah is forgiving, compassionate.

Thou mayest leave them in hope, or take them to thyself as thou willest, and if thou desirest any of those whom thou hast set aside, there will be no blame upon thee; that is the most appropriate way to ensure their comfort, and freedom from grief, and the contentment of all of them with what thou hast given them; Allah knoweth what is in your hearts; Allah hath become knowing, clement.

Women are not allowable for thee beyond (that), nor mayest thou substitute for them (other) wives, even though thou admirest their beauty; except those whom thou hast taken as slaves; Allah hath become of everything watchful.[130]

There are some commentators who see in the last of these verses a check on the size of Mohammed's

[129] For translation see Bell, *op. cit.*, II, 589 f.

[130] For translation see *ibid.*, pp. 416 f.

harem. But there are others who interpret it as limiting the *classes* of women from whom Mohammed's wives may be drawn to the classes enumerated in the preceding verses.[131] The term "wife" has been applied so far to Khadījah and to the women of Mohammed, other than concubines, for whom he provided a permanent home in the harem quarters in the court of the mosque at Medina. It is clear from the above verses and from a large and confirmatory body of traditions that Mohammed contracted marriages that were either never consummated or were of a temporary type.[132] The exact nature of these marriages is difficult to ascertain. The most that one can, with safety, say about them is that, since they mostly concerned tribal women, they were probably loose-marriage types current among the tribes and that Mohammed indulged in them largely as a bid for the support of the tribesmen.

But, whatever their nature, these marriages were an added source of vexation and jealousy to Aishah and, doubtless, also to her "sisters." It is in connection with Sūrah 33:49, that is, the first verse in the group last cited, that Aishah is reported to have said, "Verily, thy Lord hastens to do thy pleasure."[133] It is, therefore, not surprising to find her scheming to

[131] Ibn Saᶜd, VIII, 145; Baiḍāwī, II, 132 f.

[132] For a full discussion see Stern, *op. cit.*, pp. 151–57; Caetani, *op. cit.*, II[1], 476–81.

[133] Ibn Saᶜd, VIII, 112 and 141; Ibn Ḥanbal, VI, 158. But cf. Tor Andrae, *Mohammed*, trans. Menzel (New York, 1936), p. 216.

frustrate some of these marriages if and when she could.[134] Two or three stories are told of how the regular wives counseled new arrivals to refuse Mohammed's attention, adding that he would think all the more highly of them for their spirited reluctances to yield readily to his caresses. These were taught to say to Mohammed, "I take refuge with Allah from thee." The repeated use of the phrase would have undoubtedly roused Mohammed's suspicion, unless one is to assume that it was a technical formula of divorce or one implying unwillingness, for the time being at least, to consummate a marriage. But there are no other instances where it was used. Therefore, the suggestion that it was probably a pre-Islamic formula known to some, but not all, of the tribes is highly speculative. A more likely alternative is that Aishah was the inventor of the phrase and that its use was limited to one instance only, that is, in connection with Mohammed's marriage to Asmā, the daughter or sister of Nuᶜmān ibn Abī al-Jaun of the princely house of Kindah.[135]

Asmā's marriage, suggested by Nuᶜmān at the time of the delegation from Kindah, is said to have taken place in Rabīᶜ I, 9/June–July, 630. Mohammed had sent a special escort to bring her to Medina from her home in Najd. She turned out to be as beautiful as Nuᶜmān had said she was. Aishah and the harem were disturbed, not only because Mohammed's tribal mar-

[134] Cf. Ṭabarī, III, 2433.

[135] Cf. Stern, *op. cit.*, pp. 132–34; Ibn Saᶜd, VIII, 103.

riages were increasing but because this particular one brought on the scene a beautiful scion of a proud princely house. Aishah and Ḥafṣah came to help with the wedding toilet, to prepare the henna, and to comb and arrange the bride's hair. And in this friendly and "sisterly" atmosphere they instructed her to use the above formula. According to another version, it was "some women" who emphasized her royal descent and advised her to use the formula. The unsuspecting Asmā fell into the trap. For royal descent or not, Mohammed took her at her word, conceded the refuge with Allah, and ordered that she be sent back to her people. Afterward she bewailed her fate and complained that she had been the victim of deceit.[136] Harem jealousies sometimes motivated Aishah into spying on Mohammed's movements, shadowing him at times in person. One night she followed him to the cemetery and was a little ashamed of herself when she realized that Mohammed wished only to be alone and to pray.[137] Mohammed, at times, playfully chided or gently rebuked his young wife for this trait in her character.[138]

Aishah seemingly continued to suffer pangs of jealousy to the end of Mohammed's life, if we are to believe an incident placed shortly before his last illness.

[136] Ibn Saᶜd, VIII, 102–5; *Iṣābah*, III, 1153 f., IV, 442–45; cf. also Stern, *op. cit.*, pp. 132–34, 152; Caetani, *op. cit.*, II[1], 230 f., 478.

[137] Ibn Ḥanbal, VI, 76, 151, 221; Ibn ᶜAbd Rabbihi, *ᶜIqd al-Farīd* (3 vols.; Cairo, 1293/1876), I, 394.

[138] Ibn Ḥanbal, VI, 115; Bukhārī, III, 452; Yaᶜqūbī, II, 96.

Mohammed, returning from a funeral, found her complaining of a headache. His own head was throbbing too, and his mood was not a happy one.

"It would not be to your disadvantage," he said, "if you were to die before me so that I myself could wash and shroud you and pray over you and bury you."

"May that happen to another," she was quick to answer. "But that, I see," she added, "is what you wish for. You would then surely return to my apartment and there amuse yourself with some of your women."[139]

Despite Aishah's enviable position in Mohammed's harem, at least from her rival's point of view, she herself was not altogether content with her lot as a woman and wife. Motherhood, always eagerly hoped for, was denied her.[140] Traditions record a somewhat pathetic scene where the young wife, pointing out to Mohammed that all his other wives had a *kunyah* or mother designation, asks him to give her a *kunyah* too, that is, designate her as the "Mother of So-and-so." Mohammed then gave her the only *kunyah* she ever had, namely, "Umm ᶜAbd Allah," or "Mother of ᶜAbd Allah."[141] This ᶜAbd Allah was her young nephew, the son of her sister Asmā and Zubair ibn al-

[139] Ibn Saᶜd, II², 10, 24; Ibn Ḥanbal, VI, 228; Ibn Hishām, p. 1000; Ṭabarī, I, 1800.

[140] Cf. Ibn Saᶜd, II², 71 f., and Muir, *op. cit.*, p. 506.

[141] Ibn Saᶜd, VIII, 44 f.; Ibn Ḥanbal, VI, 151, 213, 260; but see *ibid.*, p. 186, and cf. Lammens, "Le Califat de Yazîd," *MFOB*, V (1912), 183, nn. 3 and 8.

ᶜAwwām, and generally believed to have been the first Moslem child to be born at Medina.[142] Between her and her "son," ᶜAbd Allah ibn al-Zubair, there grew so strong a bond of affection that there were those who quoted her as saying that she loved him more than she loved anyone else excepting Mohammed and her parents.[143]

As a wife, Aishah did not hesitate to make use of the fact that she was the only virgin bride of Mohammed. She developed an outlook that reflected the general attitude of a polygamous society much given to divorce and remarriage for both sexes. Once when Mohammed stopped in for a visit she asked where he had been that day.

"With Umm Salamah, O Fair One," he answered.

"You never seem to have enough of her company," said Aishah. Mohammed smiled and said nothing.

"Tell me," continued she, "if you were to come upon two camels, the one already pastured and the other not, which would you feed?"

"The one that has not been pastured," answered the unsuspecting Mohammed.

"I am not," she drove her point home, "like the rest of your wives. Every one of your women has been married before, except I." Again Mohammed just smiled and said nothing.[144] Little did this young

[142] Ṭabarī, I, 1263 f.; Nawawī, pp. 341 f.; Ibn ᶜAsākir, *Tārīkh al-Kabīr* (Damascus, 1329——/1911——), VII, 396.

[143] *Aghānī*, VIII, 93; cf. Bukhārī, III, 388; and see below, pp. 209 f.

[144] Ibn Saᶜd, VIII, 55.

Aishah, with her zest for a full life, then know that she was destined to outlive her one aged husband by nearly half a century to be spent in childless widowhood in a still much-married society.

It is easy enough to overemphasize the jealousies and discords inherent in the harem system, even to the point of leaving the impression that harem life, for the women at least, is one bitter and continuous competitive struggle devoid of any peace or friendship. It is equally easy to paint the master of the harem as a sensualist utterly lacking in finer family sentiments. To do this is to picture the harem system at its very worst. But no human social institution, good or bad, is ever always and everywhere at either its best or its worst. Monogamous society at its worst is not free from the prostitute or the kept mistress or the proverbial "cat-and-dog" family life. Polygamous society at anywhere near its best is not void of peace and family tenderness. We have already seen instances of comradeship if not friendship in Mohammed's harem, and the traditions are not lacking in references to some intimate and affectionate scenes between Mohammed and several of his wives. He responded readily to their request for spiritual instruction and taught some of them short individual prayers.[145] He was solicitous for their comfort and was not above attending to some of his personal needs

[145] Ibn Ḥanbal, VI, 77, 134, 146 f.; Zaid ibn ᶜAlī, *Majmūᶜāt al Fiqh*, ed. Griffini (Milan, 1919), p. 43; cf. *ᶜIqd*, I, 331.

or helping them in their simple household duties.[146] Aishah, as the favorite, doubtless enjoyed more of his personal attention than any of the others. Numerous traditions, usually traced back to Aishah herself, give some glimpses of Mohammed and Aishah as lovers.

"I know," he one day said to her, "when you are pleased with me, and when you are annoyed or angered."

"How do you know that?"

"When you are pleased, you say, 'O, Mohammed!' or 'by the Lord of Mohammed' but when you are angered you say, 'O, Messenger of Allah!' or 'by the Lord of Abraham.' "[147]

On her part she too was sensitive to his moods.[148] One day when Mohammed was busy mending his sandals and Aishah was occupied with her spinning, she saw his countenance light up. After gazing at him for a moment in either surprise or awe, she readily recited a flattering verse befitting his bright countenance. Mohammed rose and kissed her on the forehead, saying, "O, Aishah, may Allah reward you well. I am not the source of joy to you that you are to me."[149] On another occasion she readily consigned to the lower regions those who troubled or annoyed him.[150] She was concerned for his physical comfort

[146] Ibn Saᶜd, I², 90 f.; Bukhārī, III, 489; cf. Dermenghem, *op. cit.*, pp. 165 f.

[147] Ibn Saᶜd, VIII, 47, 55; Ibn Ḥanbal, VI, 30, 61, 213; Bukhārī, III, 452.

[148] Cf. Ibn Ḥanbal, VI, 159.

[149] Abū Nuᶜaim, II, 45 f.

[150] Ibn Ḥanbal, VI, 175.

and health, as seen, for instance, in her cautioning him against exposure to the Meccan sun.[151] She good-naturedly took him to task if she thought he was pampering himself too much; but when he was sick she nursed and doctored him.[152] She delighted in waiting on him and in anointing his hair with his favorite perfume.[153] She rejoiced in such intimacies as washing in the same bowl and drinking, lover-like, out of the same cup.[154] Woman-like, she teased her beloved[155] to declare his love.

"What is your love for me like?"

"Like a (firm) knot in a rope."

"And what is that like?"

"Always the same."[156]

Mohammed, it is believed, had premonitions of his approaching end. He was at Maimūnah's house when he first realized that the sickness which had overtaken him was more than a passing ailment.[157] Some of his wives visited him while he was yet in Maimūnah's house. Presently he began to ask where he was that day, where he was to be on the morrow, and where on the day after. The harem realized that he was trying

[151] Balādhurī, *Futūḥ al-Buldān*, ed. de Goeje (Lugduni Batavorum, 1886), p. 43.

[152] Ibn Saᶜd, II², 11, 15, 29; Ibn Ḥanbal, VI, 215 and 67; Abū Nuᶜaim, II, 50.

[153] Ibn Ḥanbal, VI, 186 and 272.

[154] Ibn Saᶜd, VIII, 43; Ibn Ḥanbal, VI, 123 and 64.

[155] Ibn Ḥanbal, VI, 210.

[156] Abū Nuᶜaim, II, 44.

[157] Ibn Saᶜd, II², 10, 24, 29 f., 31; Ṭabarī, I, 1800 f. (but p. 1799 has Zainab instead).

to figure out the day of Aishah's "turn." Their surmise was confirmed when he asked, as a special favor, that he be allowed to retire to and stay in Aishah's apartment.[158] It was therefore in her house that he lived his few remaining days, as it was in her arms that he breathed his last (Rabīᶜ I, 11/June, 632). The young wife did not spare herself in nursing him. His death agony left a lasting impression on her. When she realized it was all over, she gently placed his head on a pillow and herself joined the weeping women.[159] Later she expressed a wish that she and the rest of his wives be allowed to wash the body and prepare it for burial, but in this she was overruled by the men of the family.[160] These first prayed over the body, and then Mohammed's wives performed the same rite.[161] Abū Bakr settled the question of the burial place by recalling that Mohammed had said that a prophet is buried where he expires.[162] So came Aishah to share her living-quarters with the dead Mohammed, while her apartment at Medina came in time to be a most sacred spot in all Islam, second only to the Kaᶜbah at Mecca.

This is as good a place as any to raise the question

[158] Ibn Saᶜd, II², 30; Bukhārī, III, 189; Ṭabarī, I, 1801; Ibn Ḥanbal, VI, 219.

[159] Ibn Saᶜd, II, 30; Ibn Hishām, 1011 f.; Ṭabarī, I, 1812–14; Bukhārī, III, 187; Ibn Ḥanbal, VI, 219.

[160] Ibn Saᶜd, II², 60; Ṭabarī, I, 1831.

[161] Ibn Saᶜd, II², 46 f., 68–70; Ṭabarī, I, 1805.

[162] Ibn Saᶜd, II², 71 f.; but see *ibid.*, p. 35.

of Aishah's early influence directly on Mohammed and indirectly on the political course of early Islam. The Moslem traditions, resentful for the most part of women leadership, have if anything understated Aishah's influence except perhaps in the decidedly major role she played in the Battle of the Camel. Western scholars, on the other hand, much impressed —and rightly so—by her role in that battle, have yielded to the temptation to place her earlier influence near that high level, especially where the interests of her father were concerned. These seem to forget the tender age at which Aishah entered Mohammed's harem and the fact that she was but eighteen years old at the time of his death. They seem also to have failed to realize that of the two, that is, Mohammed and Abū Bakr, the first was by far the gentler with her and the more considerate of her wishes. It is, therefore, not likely that Aishah deliberately did anything contrary to Mohammed's desires primarily in the interests of her father and his two political aids, ᶜUmar ibn al-Khaṭṭāb and Abū ᶜUbaidah ᶜĀmir ibn ᶜAbd Allah ibn al-Jarrāḥ, the trio christened by Lammens as "the Triumvirate." Had Aishah, that early, been indeed the master-intriguer and accomplished spy that, for instance, Lammens, and following him Caetani and others,[163] would have one believe she was, then it is difficult to see why both Abū Bakr and ᶜUmar failed to find

[163] "Le 'Triumvirat,' " *op. cit.*, pp. 120–23, 128, 131 f.; Caetani, *op. cit.*, III¹, 125 f., n. 4; V, 480 n. 1.

further outlets for her talents. For the fact of the matter is that few events of any political significance are associated with her during their successive caliphates. To assume that there was no need for her talents in their time is to oversimplify the momentous years that followed the death of Mohammed—years in which everyone that was, or thought he was, somebody in the new community strove to climb into the fast-moving and much-promising political wagon. Among the would-be climbers were several of Aishah's friends and relatives, a few of whom were not only ambitious but clever and calculating. These were not men to overlook the possible influence, for or against them, that a clever and intriguing Aishah could have exerted, even if but indirectly, over either Abū Bakr or ʿUmar or both.

Inasmuch as Lammens has gone as far as, if not indeed farther than, most Western scholars in painting a picture of an actively intriguing Aishah this early in her career, it became necessary to examine his materials very carefully.[164] This examination revealed that, while Lammens was careful to emphasize that Aishah was Mohammed's *best* beloved, he had a tendency to forget that she was not his *only* beloved. It could, therefore, not have been so simple a matter for Aishah, best-beloved though she was, to greatly influence, let alone dominate, Mohammed. It seems that even for such private activities as following Mohammed's example of temporary seclusion for prayer

[164] See preceding note.

or visiting her sick father, she had first to ask and secure Mohammed's permission.[165] Lammens, furthermore, credits Aishah with a "mania for spying" and cites as proof an incident where she listened in on a conversation between Mohammed and ᶜUthmān ibn ᶜAffān and an incident or two where she followed Mohammed to determine his destination. He discredits harem jealousy as the main motive for this activity of hers and prefers to see in it proof of determined political intrigue on her part.[166] That Father Lammens should fail to estimate correctly the great motive powers of harem jealousy is perhaps understandable. But that he should be so readily satisfied with an incident or two of this sort as proof of a "mania" for political spying is difficult to understand. He may have had in mind other instances similar to those he does mention, for a few others can be found. There was, for instance, the time when Aishah, sensing that something had disturbed Mohammed, followed him to the door and listened to a speech he made outside.[167] There was also the occasion of the news of the death of Jaᶜfar ibn Abī Ṭālib (8/629) when she was peeping through the (curtain) door, watching Mohammed handle the situation and strive to calm the weeping women.[168] Again there was the time when

[165] Ibn Ḥanbal, VI, 65, 84, 226.

[166] "Le 'Triumvirat,'" *op. cit.*, p. 122 and n. 2.

[167] Ibn Ḥanbal, VI, 159.

[168] *Ibid.*, pp. 58 f.; Ibn Saᶜd, IV, 27.

she heard Mohammed talking to his court poet, Ḥassān ibn Thābit.[169]

Do such incidents as the above, however, necessarily prove a mania for spying and political intrigue? To be in a position to answer this question, one must look not at Aishah only but at Aishah *and* her surroundings. What, then, are the surroundings in which one finds the true daughter of Abū Bakr and the jealous beloved of Mohammed? She was, to begin with, subject to the *ḥijāb*, or seclusion. She lived in a small one-room apartment in which Mohammed frequently received his friends. This same apartment opened onto the court of the mosque, where most of Mohammed's interviews and speeches took place within seeing and hearing distance. Under these circumstances what would anyone in Aishah's position do? Sit in the corner of the apartment and stay put? Go blind and deaf to the scenes of life surrounding her—scenes in which her own Mohammed played the major leading role? Take away the *ḥijāb* from this view of Aishah and her surroundings, and all these "spying" episodes of listening or peeping from behind the curtain appear in their true light. They are not the doings of a redoubtable intriguer but the normal reactions of a young and lively woman abnormally restricted by recent seclusion. That Aishah was at times in a position to pass out information, consciously or otherwise, of political significance to her father is very likely; but that she deliberately set out to spy

[169] *Aghānī*, IV, 6.

on Mohammed with that aim in view is highly improbable.

It is indeed significant that Lammens himself cites but one specific instance of what he might call the fruits of Aishah's espionage. The episode, as the early sources at my command give it, was as follows: Mohammed had decided, apparently without consulting Abū Bakr, to undertake an expedition against Mecca. Keeping his destination secret, he gave orders to prepare for the march. Abū Bakr, no doubt sensing that something was in the air, called on Aishah, whom he found busy preparing provisions for the march.

"O daughter, did the Messenger of Allah order these preparations?"

"Yes, get ready yourself," came her brief answer.

"Where do you see him headed for?"

"By Allah, I know not," was the unenlightening response. Presently Mohammed himself told the people what Abū Bakr wished to know, namely, that the expedition was to be against Mecca.[170] Lammens, disregarding this oft-repeated account, prefers a questionable one which depicts Aishah as divulging to Abū Bakr Mohammed's secret plan to attack Mecca. He, furthermore, uses the incident as a typical example of how Aishah was given to rob Mohammed of his secrets to satisfy the curiosity of her father![171]

[170] Ibn Hishām, p. 808; Ṭabarī, I, 1625; Wāqidī, *Kitāb al-Maghāzī*, trans. Weldhausen (Berlin, 1882), p. 325; Tor Andrae, *op. cit.*, p. 230.

[171] "Le 'Triumvirat,' " *op. cit.*, p. 128. His sources are Ibn Hishām (p. 808) and *Muntakhab Kanz al-ᶜUmmāl* (IV, 149), a sixteenth- or post-sixteenth-century work (cf. Brocklemann, *Geschichte*, II, 384 f. and 151,

Other incidents generally accepted as reflecting Aishah's intrigue and influence in the political interests of her father are those associated with Mohammed's last sickness and death. Here, before going any further, one must again look at Aishah's surroundings. It is true that Mohammed spent his illness, about a fortnight's duration at the most, in her apartment. This, however, does not mean that Aishah and

No. 153). However, the passage in question is no doubt that to be found in the original and unabridged sixteenth-century work of Muttaqī, *Kanz al-ᶜUmmāl* (Hyderabad, 1894–97), V, 302. This late work of compilation from the Ḥadīth states that Mohammed confided his destination to Aishah but ordered her not to reveal it to anyone—a detail likewise found in the sixteenth-century biography of Mohammed, *Al-Sīrah al-Ḥalabīyah* (3 vols.; Cairo, 1911), III, 86. The *Kanz al-ᶜUmmāl* then describes Abū Bakr's visit to Aishah, who is led to reveal Mecca as Mohammed's destination—a detail not confirmed by the *Al-Sīrah al-Ḥalabīyah*, which at this point follows the earlier accounts. Muttaqī credits the account he reports to Ibn Abī Shaibah, who in turn received it from one Yazīd ibn Hārūn. Abū Shaibah Ibrahīm ibn ᶜUthmān was a judge in Wāsiṭ and a *rāwī*, or traditionist, who died in the reign of Hārūn al-Rashīd. As a traditionist he was specifically characterized as "weak," that is, unreliable. Yazīd ibn Hārūn received traditions from him. This in turn casts reflections on Yazīd as a reliable traditionist (cf. Ibn Saᶜd, VI, 267). Abū Shaibah had a son, Mohammed, who, so far as I can find out, did not go in for traditions. Mohammed's two sons, Abū Bakr ᶜAbd Allah and Abū al-Ḥasan ᶜUthmān, and a grandson, Mohammed ibn ᶜUthmān (d. A.H. 297), were traditionists of the Kūfan school (cf. *ibid.*, p. 288; Wüstenfeld, *Die Geschichtschreiber der Araber* [Göttingen, 1882], p. 29, No. 86). Muttaqī does not specify which of these three is the Ibn Abī Shaibah of his account. However, judging by the fact that Yazīd ibn Hārūn is the immediate informant and also by the works attributed to Abū Bakr ᶜAbd Allah (d. A.H. 235), the latter is most probably the Ibn Abī Shaibah in question (cf. *Fihrist*, pp. 34 and 229; Mohammed Shafīᶜ, *Analytical Indices to the Kitāb al-ᶜIḳd al-Farīd* [Calcutta, 1935], I, 454). The account, then, which Lammens preferred turns out to be late, based on unreliable traditionists, and originating from the Kūfan school, which school, generally favorable to ᶜAlī, had not much love for Aishah.

Mohammed had anything like the privacy that might on first thought present itself to a modern Western mind. In the East of even today a sickroom is the scene of an almost continuous stream of all sorts of visitors by day, while close relatives stay and take turns as helpers by night. There is no reason to believe these customs were any different in the time of Mohammed. As long as Mohammed could still move about or sit up in comfort, he met his visitors or talked to the large crowds in the court of the mosque from the threshold of Aishah's apartment. When he took a turn for the worse and his temperature mounted higher and higher, the "family members" were there to render service as best they knew how. But Mohammed did have his few moments of relief from both visitors and pain. It must have been during one or more of these that he expressed a desire to see some of his friends. According to what is obviously an Umayyad version of such an episode, Mohammed's desire met with either suggestions from Aishah or with a collective inquiry from Aishah and others as to whom he wished to see. "Shall we call Abū Bakr?" they suggested. Mohammed made no answer.

"Shall we call ʿUmar?" Again no answer.

"Shall we call ʿAlī?" Still no answer.

"Shall we call ʿUthmān?"

"Yes," at last spoke Mohammed. So they sent for ʿUthmān, with whom Mohammed had a private conversation, during which ʿUthmān's countenance registered a visible change.[172]

[172] Ibn Ḥanbal, VI, 52, 214 f.

But according to what is as obviously an ᶜAbbāsid version of this or a similar occasion during Mohammed's illness, Mohammed expressly called for ᶜAlī, but Aishah ignored the request and suggested instead her father Abū Bakr. Next Ḥafṣah suggested ᶜUmar, and Maimūnah suggested ᶜAbbās. Though all three were called, yet ᶜAlī was not. Mohammed noted the latter's absence but said nothing.[173] One wonders why Fāṭimah and Umm Salamah failed to see that ᶜAlī was called! It is clear that neither of these late and partisan accounts are telling the truth, the whole truth, and nothing but the truth. It is equally clear that one cannot tell with absolute certainty just what actually took place on such occasions. But the most likely probabilities are that Mohammed himself indicated whom he wished to see at the same time that the leading members of his harem, Aishah included, strove to have some of their own folks on hand.

Another important incident of the sickroom in which Aishah is generally credited with watching out for the political interests of her father is Mohammed's delegation of Abū Bakr to lead in the public prayer in the mosque. Here again the traditions give different versions of the story. In all versions it was Mohammed who wished Abū Bakr to lead in prayers. According to most versions, Aishah, though not always suggesting anyone else, tried to persuade Mohammed to excuse Abū Bakr from that duty on the plea of his weak voice and tender disposition which

[173] *Ibid.*, I, 356; Ṭabarī, I, 1810 f.; Bukhārī, I, 175.

would cause him to break down and weep.[174] According to one version, Aishah suggested "some one other than Abū Bakr";[175] but, according to others, she definitely suggested ᶜUmar.[176] According to still others, she enlisted the aid of Ḥafṣah to excuse Abū Bakr and to suggest ᶜUmar. Mohammed lost patience, called them "Joseph's companions," and insisted that Abū Bakr lead the prayers. Ḥafṣah then remarked to Aishah, "I never get anything good through you."[177] According to a number of traditions, Aishah's real motive for all this was not the reason she gave Mohammed but rather a desire to spare her father the disfavor of the public, who, she felt, would resent Abū Bakr or anyone else who replaced Mohammed in the leadership of prayers.[178] In one version she is represented as saying she would rather have ᶜUmar than her father exposed to this public disfavor.[179]

There is, on the other hand, a tradition which would seem to indicate that it was not so much what

[174] Ṭabarī, I, 1811; Ibn Saᶜd, III, 126; Bukhārī, I, 185; Ibn Ḥanbal IV, 412; V, 361; VI, 96, 159.

[175] Ibn Ḥanbal, VI, 229.

[176] *Ibid.*, I, 356; VI, 270; Ibn Saᶜd II², 18 f.; Bukhārī, I, 176, 185 f.

[177] Ibn Saᶜd, III¹, 127; Ibn Ḥanbal, I, 209, VI, 202, 224; Bukhārī, I, 176, 187, IV, 426.

[178] E.g., Ibn Hishām, p. 1008; Ibn Ḥanbal, VI, 34; Bukhārī, I, 185 f., III, 187 f.; cf. also reference in n. 176 above, and Muir, *op. cit.*, p. 486, n. 4.

[179] Ibn Saᶜd, II², 24.

Mohammed wished or what Aishah said as what ᶜUmar and Abū Bakr themselves felt and said about the matter that finally settled the leadership of the prayer on Abū Bakr. Mohammed sent word to Abū Bakr to lead the large crowd gathered in the mosque in prayer. Abū Bakr turned to ᶜUmar and asked him to lead instead, but ᶜUmar replied, "You are worthier of that (leadership than I)." That seems to have settled the matter, and Abū Bakr lead the congregation.[180] Other traditions add that Abū Bakr did actually break down and was overcome by weeping and that someone came to inform Mohammed and to ask who should then lead, when Ḥafṣah took it upon herself to send word that her father, ᶜUmar, should lead. No sooner did Mohammed hear ᶜUmar's voice raised in prayer than he, much disturbed, gave orders to stop him and have Abū Bakr lead.[181] But, according to still another version, Mohammed gave orders to have "someone" lead. The messenger told ᶜUmar to lead, which he did until Mohammed sent to stop him. ᶜUmar had understood that the messenger came to him expressly on Mohammed's order. The messenger, in turn, explained that, seeing Abū Bakr was absent, he judged ᶜUmar worthier of the leadership than any of the others.[182]

What is one, as far as Aishah was concerned, to

[180] *Ibid.*, p. 19; Ibn Ḥanbal, II, 52; Bukhārī, I, 179.

[181] Ibn Saᶜd, II², 21, ll. 11 ff.

[182] *Ibid.*, pp. 20 f.; Ibn Hishām, p. 1009.

make of all these varied and in several instances contradictory traditions? The answer is linked with yet another question, namely, what significance, if any, did the leadership in prayer have? Did it actually have in the Year 11 the all-important significance of political successorship that these traditions and later practices give it? If it did not, which is a possibility, then Aishah's fears and actions have no political significance. If it did, which is again possible, then Aishah's actions were decidedly detrimental to her father's interests, not because she wished ᶜUmar to succeed Mohammed, but because she had so woefully underestimated her father's abilities and misjudged the outlook and temper of the people. Again regardless of whether this leadership in prayer had or had not a political significance, Aishah's wishes concerning her father were neither granted by Mohammed nor carried out by Abū Bakr. Is this, then, the redoubtable intriguer who enjoyed the confidence of her father and who completely dominated the sickly and infirm Mohammed?[183] Lammens' exaggerated estimate of Aishah's political influence in the last years of Mohammed's life is but a reflection of his clearly exaggerated estimate of the power of the "Triumvirate" over Mohammed himself.

We have followed the child Aishah and seen her as the carefree and playful girl-wife of Mohammed. We have watched her as she grew into the lovely and be-

[183] Cf. Lammens, "Le 'Triumvirat,' " *op. cit.*, pp. 122 f. and 117, n. 4.

loved but jealous and aggressive first mistress of his harem. That all-engrossing role was ended with the death of the prophet. Compelled to lifelong widowhood, the young, active, and intelligent "Mother of the Believers" will turn her energies and talents more and more into political channels, until, for a time at least, she will come to dominate the political situation with spirit and energy second to none.

II

Mother of the Believers

I

THE political atmosphere, tense enough during Mohammed's last illness, reached a climax with his death. The Medinans, resenting their secondary role, thought this was their opportunity to assert themselves against the Meccans who had entrenched themselves too well in the city so hospitable to the prophet. The Hāshimites, centering their hopes on ᶜAlī, largely because he was Mohammed's son-in-law, aspired to the heirship of the prophet, hoping thereby to supplant the aristocratic clans of the Umayyads and Makhzūmites as leaders of the Arabs. But Abū Bakr and ᶜUmar, for long Mohammed's staunchest supporters and outspoken counselors, were bent on retaining their advantageous position. How they succeeded in doing this by bold, well-timed, and united action is to be read in any good history of early Islam.

What part, if any, Aishah played in the eventual election of her father is nowhere clearly defined. The traditions credit her with contradictory statements. According to some of these, she claimed that Mohammed left no successor but added that, had he done so, he would have certainly appointed either Abū Bakr or ᶜUmar.[1] Such a statement is a very probable one as coming from Aishah and is in keeping with her reactions to Mohammed's appointment of Abū Bakr or ᶜUmar to the leadership in prayers, as it is also in keeping with the respective rank generally accorded these men in Islam.[2] But, according to another group of traditions, she is made to state that Mohammed had said his successors were to be Abū Bakr, ᶜUmar, and Abū ᶜUbaidah.[3] It is very improbable that Aishah, or anyone else for that matter, would have voiced so cut and dried a solution of imposed succession to the still election-minded democratic Arabs. Such statements are more likely to have been made by Aishah, if at all, *after* the election of her father either in further justification of that event or in support of Abū Bakr's appointment of ᶜUmar as his successor or even in support of the teamwork between ᶜUmar and Abū ᶜUbaidah. It is perhaps pertinent to note here that Aishah is not associated any more definitely or positively with the succession of

[1] Ibn Ḥanbal, *Musnad* (6 vols.; Cairo, 1313/1895–96), VI, 63.

[2] E.g., Bukhārī, *Ṣaḥīḥ*, ed. Krehl (4 vols.; Leiden, 1862–1908), II, 419 f.; cf. Wensinck, *A Handbook of Early Mohammedan Traditions* (Leiden, 1927), p. 234 for other references.

[3] E.g., Ibn Saᶜd, *Ṭabaqāt* (9 vols.; Leiden, 1905–40), III[1], 128; Abū Zakariyā Yaḥyā al-Nawawī, *Kitāb Tahdhīb al-Asmā* ("Biographical Dictionary"), ed. Wüstenfeld (Göttingen, 1842–47), pp. 664–66; cf. Henri Lammens, "Le 'Triumvirat' ...," *MFOB*, IV (1910), 113–44; Tirmidhī, *Ṣaḥīḥ* (13 vols.; Cairo, 1931–34), XIII, 126.

ᶜUmar than this type of traditions implies. Negatively, her influence was doubtless felt in her effective challenge of ᶜAlī's claims to the succession based on supposed statements of Mohammed made in his last illness to and in favor of ᶜAlī. Her point was that she had been with Mohammed to the last and had not heard him make any such statements.[4]

The young widow had her own immediate problems to face and adjustments to make, now that Mohammed was no more. She, together with the rest of Mohammed's widows, went through a period of mourning, and all of them seem to have continued to live in their small mosque apartments.[5] Mohammed, it is believed, made no specific provisions for his widows, and the little he left was to go for charity. This need not mean that the prophet's wives were left destitute. Some of them had means of their own, and others had ways of earning some money. Furthermore, neither their families nor, failing these, the Moslem community would leave these Mothers of the Believers in any real want. Nevertheless, they, like Mohammed's daughter Fāṭimah, expected to be heirs to some of Mohammed's sources of revenue. Abū Bakr decided the question adversely in Fāṭimah's case and won her bitter resentment and public denunciation. She refused to speak to him, while her husband, ᶜAlī, took the oath of allegiance to Abū Bakr only after her death, which took place a few

[4] E.g., Ibn Saᶜd, II², 49; Bukhārī, III, 191 f.; Ibn Ḥanbal, VI, 32.

[5] Ibn Saᶜd, VIII, 159 f.; for the apartment cf. *ibid.*, pp. 117–20.

months after that of Mohammed.[6] Aishah in all probability approved and upheld her father's decision, for when the rest of Mohammed's widows sent ᶜUthmān to Abū Bakr to ask for their inheritance, Aishah chided her "sisters" and reminded them that Mohammed had said what he left was to go to charity in the service of the community and its leader. Her "sisters" therefore refrained from further action.[7] Aishah herself was well taken care of by her father, who had allotted her some lands in the ᶜĀliyah quarters of Medina and in the district of Baḥrain.[8]

Abū Bakr's reign (A.H. 11–13/A.D. 632–34), however, was too short to allow Aishah to establish herself as a major factor in the politics of the day. Yet, in their personal relationships, father and daughter seem to have drawn very close together, for it was she who nursed him during his last illness as she had nursed Mohammed. It was to her that he intrusted his last wishes concerning the disposal of some small public funds and property, as it was also to her care that he committed the interests of her brothers and sisters, charging her to share what she had received from him with these, the rest of his children.[9] Abū

[6] *Ibid.*, II², 82; Ṭabarī, *Tārīkh* ("Annales"), ed. de Goeje (15 vols.; Lugduni Batavorum, 1879–1901), I, 1825 f.; cf. Lammens, *Fāṭima et filles de Mahomet* (Rome, 1912), pp. 112–14.

[7] Balādhurī, *Futūḥ al-Buldān*, ed. de Goeje (Lugduni Batavorum, 1886), p. 30.

[8] Ibn Saᶜd, III¹, 138.

[9] *Ibid.*, pp. 136–40, 149; Ibn ᶜAbd Rabbihi, *ᶜIqd al-Farīd* (3 vols.; Cairo, 1293/1876), II, 4, 252 f.

Bakr, therefore, seems to have sized her up as the most able and dependable of his offspring. Touching details are told of her grief at the time of his passing-away. She and the rest of the women wailed loudly when at last the end came. But ᶜUmar thought such expression of grief—said to have been condemned by Mohammed—was ungodly. He, therefore, took immediate steps to stop it, though this involved physical rough handling of Abū Bakr's wailing sister.[10] Aishah, nevertheless, continued to indulge in this custom, though eventually she conceded ᶜUmar's view on the matter to be correct.[11] The departed caliph was, in accordance with his own request, buried in the floor of Aishah's apartment close to where Mohammed had been laid.[12] Standing at the tomb, she paid her tribute to her father in terms of glowing praise.[13]

Bereft of husband and father in such quick succession, Aishah was from now on to rely largely on her own resources for whatever influence she might wish to exercise in public affairs. Her relationships with ᶜUmar seem to have been for the most part cordial and co-operative. To start out with, she must have well pleased ᶜUmar, the strict financial steward, when she carried out her father's wishes in relinquishing two milch camels to the state and also in replacing some funds said to have been drawn by him from the

[10] Ibn Saᶜd, III[1], 148; Ṭabarī, I, 2131 f.

[11] Ibn Saᶜd, III[1], 251, 263.

[12] *Ibid.*, p. 149.

[13] ᶜ*Iqd*, II, 8.

state treasury.[14] Nevertheless, she did not hesitate to demand from ᶜUmar some property that she felt belonged to the family. Her half-brother, ᶜAbd Allah, had married the beautiful ᶜĀtikah bint Zaid, for whose company he neglected his private and public affairs so much that Abū Bakr had ordered him to divorce her. ᶜAbd Allah complied, but his grief was so great that his father took pity on him and allowed him to take her back before the divorce was final.[15] ᶜAbd Allah died before his father as a result of wounds received in the siege of Ṭāʾif, but not before he had settled some property on ᶜĀtikah on condition that she should not remarry after his death. ᶜUmar, who wished to marry her, suggested she return the property to the family of Abū Bakr and so be free to remarry. But perhaps ᶜĀtikah was not so ready to part with any of her wealth, since it was *after* her marriage to ᶜUmar that Aishah claimed and probably received the property involved.[16] The marriage is reported as taking place in A.H. 12 (A.D. 633), that is, in Abū Bakr's reign.[17] Aishah's demand for the return of the property probably took place early in ᶜUmar's cal-

[14] Ibn Saᶜd, III[1], 138; Balādhurī, *Ansāb*, V (Jerusalem, 1936), 88.

[15] *Kitāb al-Aghānī* (20 vols.; Cairo, 1285/1868), XVI, 133; Ibn Ḥajar, *Kitāb al-Iṣābah* (Calcutta, 1873), II, 696 f.; IV, 685 f.; see *EI*, I, 505, art. "ᶜĀtika."

[16] Ibn Saᶜd, VIII, 193–95; *Aghānī*, XVI, 134; cf. Caetani, *Annali dell' Islam* (10 vols.; Milan, 1905–26), II[2], 1236 f.

[17] Ṭabarī, I, 2077; Ibn al-Athīr, *Al-Kāmil fī al-Tārīkh* ("Chronicon"), ed. C. J. Tornberg (14 vols.; Upsaliae et Lugduni Batavorum, 1851–76), II, 307.

iphate. The incident is significant in that it is illustrative of Aishah's energy in looking after the family interests.

ᶜĀtikah's subsequent history shows her to have been a determined woman. It also throws some light on ᶜUmar's harem; for it shows him to have been not only harsh with his wives but also jealous of any attention paid them. When Abū Mūsā al-Ashᶜarī presented ᶜĀtikah with a small Persian carpet, ᶜUmar's rage would not be appeased until he had struck ᶜĀtikah with it and had Abū Mūsā belabored and then brought into his presence, when, throwing the offending carpet at his head, he berated him soundly for daring to make a present to any of his wives.[18] ᶜĀtikah, nevertheless, seems to have had her own way in some respects with the stern ᶜUmar, for despite his disapproval she persisted in attending public prayers at the mosque and was present there at the time of his assassination.[19] When her period of waiting was over, she married Zubair ibn al-ᶜAwwām on condition that she never be beaten and that she be permitted to continue her attendance at the mosque. The condition, however, did her no good, for Zubair tricked her into giving up the mosque-going habit. He saw to it that she was somewhat roughly handled on one occasion, whereupon she herself, bewailing the ill-bred public, preferred to pray at home.[20] When Zubair fell

[18] Ibn Saᶜd, III[1], 222.

[19] *Ibid.*, VIII, 195.

[20] *Iṣābah*, IV, 687.

in the Battle of the Camel, the people of Medina began to say, "Let him, who wishes to be a martyr, marry ᶜĀtikah." Her fourth husband was Ḥusain ibn ᶜAlī, who was martyred at Karbalā.[21]

A love affair of ᶜAbd al-Raḥmān, Aishah's older and only full brother,[22] gave ᶜUmar a chance to please the son of Abū Bakr at the same time that it demanded some of Aishah's attention. ᶜAbd al-Raḥmān, while in Syria, had chanced to see a Ghassānid maid, Lailā bint al-Jūdī, to whom he had promptly lost his heart. ᶜUmar arranged it so that she fell to ᶜAbd al-Raḥmān's lot after the fall of Damascus. The young man became so enamored of her that Aishah saw fit to caution him. Later, he came so to hate the girl that Aishah once again took him to task for going to such extremes of love and hate. Lailā in her distress had turned to Aishah for help, and the latter persuaded her brother to send the unhappy girl back to her people.[23] Aishah's influence in the marital affairs of this brother was not limited to a negative role, for it was she who had arranged his marriage to Quraibah, the divorced wife of ᶜUmar ibn al-Khaṭṭāb and the beautiful sister of the equally beautiful Umm Salamah who had so won the heart of Mohammed. ᶜAbd al-Raḥmān was made to feel that, were it not for Aishah, the hand of Quraibah would have been refused him. He, therefore, offered to di-

[21] Ibn Saᶜd, III[1], 79; *Aghānī*, XVI, 136.

[22] Ibn Saᶜd, II[2], 30; III[1], 120; Ṭabarī, I, 2134; Nawawī, pp. 377 f.

[23] *Aghānī*, XVI, 94 f.; Balādhurī, *Futūh*, pp. 62 f.; *Iṣābah*, II, 979.

vorce Quraibah, but she chose to stay with her husband.[24]

ᶜAbd al-Raḥmān does not play the leading role that one would expect from the oldest son of Abū Bakr and the full brother of Aishah. He did, it is true, get a wrong start in the new community. He had opposed the new faith and fought against his father and his father's prophet in the battles of Badr and Uḥud and was converted to Islam only at the time of the Treaty of Ḥudaibīyah.[25] In traditions, usually traced back to Aishah, ᶜAbd al-Raḥmān appears at the sick-bed of Mohammed, who had wished to have him, together with Abū Bakr, draw up his will.[26] He does not seem to have distinguished himself in the cause of Islam until in the reign of his father when he accompanied Khālid ibn al-Walīd on the expedition against Musailimah and fought valiantly at the Battle of ᶜAqrabah.[27] His wrong start, however, was not in itself sufficient to relegate him to the secondary role he plays in politics and the affairs of state. His main difficulty was a fault of character, for he was self-indulgent and on the whole easygoing.[28] Abū Bakr must have been well aware of this when he passed him over to intrust the welfare of his family to the more capa-

[24] Mālik ibn Anas, *Muwaṭṭā*ᵓ (Cairo, A.H. 1339), II, 37 f.; cf. Ibn Saᶜd, VIII, 191 f.; Ṭabarī, I, 2733; Ibn al-Athīr, III, 41; *Iṣābah*, IV, 751 f.

[25] Nawawī, pp. 377 f.; *Iṣābah*, II, 978.

[26] Ibn Ṣaᶜd, III¹, 127 f.

[27] Nawawī, p. 377; *Iṣābah*, II, 979.

[28] Cf. Lammens, "Le 'Triumvirat,' " *op. cit.*, p. 123 and n. 4.

ble and energetic Aishah. In the years to come brother and sister would have some differences of opinion in family matters; but to the end of ᶜAbd al-Raḥmān's days Aishah would rush to his support against any outsider. ᶜAbd al-Raḥmān's weakness was, in a measure, ᶜUmar's opportunity; for there were those who believed that, had Abū Bakr's sons (but Mohammed was yet too young) been like Aishah, "neither much nor little would have befallen ᶜUmar."[29]

An incident indicative of the good will and co-operation existing between ᶜUmar and Aishah concerned her young charge and half-sister, Umm Kulthūm. Some time, presumably in the Year 17 (A.D. 638), ᶜUmar, who was then in his sixties, asked Aishah for the hand of this sister, who was hardly more than a baby, having been born in the Year 13, soon after the death of Abū Bakr.[30] Aishah readily consented to the proposal, which, considering Umm Kulthūm's tender age, could have involved no more than a promise to reserve her for ᶜUmar until she became of marriageable age. The traditions at this point tell a curious tale full of improbabilities. According to these, Umm Kulthūm herself protested the arrangement, threatened to wail at the tomb of Mohammed if Aishah forced her hand, and brazenly proclaimed she had no use for the harsh and stingy ᶜUmar, caliph though he was, but wished for a youth that would

[29] Cf. Lammens, "Moᶜâwia Ier," *MFOB*, II (1907), 112, n. 4.

[30] Ibn Saᶜd, III[1], 138, 149; Ṭabarī, I, 2135.

shower her with this world's goods.[31] Aishah was in a dilemma. She confided her troubles to either ᶜAmr ibn al-ᶜĀṣ[32] or Mughīrah ibn Shuᶜbah,[33] who undertook to dissuade ᶜUmar from marrying Umm Kulthūm. The argument put before ᶜUmar was: Umm Kulthūm was too young and raised by Aishah in tenderness and ease. You, on the other hand, are harsh; we fear you and are unable to change a single trait of your character. What if she should disagree with you or disobey you in anything and you overpower or assault her? You will then have treated the children of Abū Bakr in a manner unbefitting to you. Let me lead you to a better match. There is Umm Kulthūm, the daughter of ᶜAlī and Fāṭimah. By marrying her you become related to the Messenger of Allah. ᶜUmar saw the double point of this argument. It was now his turn to be in a dilemma. "But what of Aishah?" he asked. "Leave that to me," said his adviser. So the proposed marriage was called off, and ᶜUmar married Umm Kulthūm the daughter of ᶜAlī.

It is inconceivable that a child of four could, by her threats, have forced Aishah's hand in the matter. If Umm Kulthūm indeed uttered the protests she is credited with, she must have done so toward the end of ᶜUmar's reign when she would have been about ten years of age and capable, with perhaps some tutoring,

[31] Ṭabarī, I, 2734; Ibn ᶜAsākir, *Tārīkh al-Kabīr* (Damascus, 1329——/1911——), VII, 79 f.; cf. Lammens, "Le 'Triumvirat,' " *op. cit.*, p. 120 n.

[32] Ṭabarī, I, 2734; Ibn al-Athīr, III, 42; Ibn ᶜAsākir, VII, 79 f.

[33] ᶜ*Iqd*, III, 275 f.; *Aghānī*, XIV, 144.

of taking such an attitude. In that case ʿUmar's and Aishah's agreement, if it was in any way connected with the marriage of ʿUmar to the daughter of ʿAlī in the Year 17,[34] must have been in good standing for several years. The *Aghānī* version of this story differs considerably from the rest. It does not record Umm Kulthūm's reactions and protests. According to it, it was Aishah, who, though she had given her consent to ʿUmar's proposal, was nevertheless concerned about the fate of her little sister and wished for her an easier life than she was likely to have with ʿUmar. When Mughīrah broached the subject to ʿUmar, the latter immediately suspected Aishah's reluctance and released her from her promise.[35] There is nothing improbable about this version of the story. Furthermore, it is in keeping with Aishah's two constantly dominant objectives, namely, timely but controlled co-operation with the strong powers that be and the welfare of the members of her family both individually and as a clan.

Aishah does not seem to have in any way opposed ʿUmar's generally severe attitude toward the women, his attempt to restrict them to their homes, and his efforts to keep them from attending at the mosques. She is, on the contrary, credited with saying, "Were Mohammed to see what we today see of the women and their behavior or condition, he would prohibit them from going to the mosque."[36] The "today" of

[34] Ṭabarī, I, 2529; Ibn al-Athīr, II, 419.

[35] *Aghānī*, XIV, 144 f.

[36] Ibn Ḥanbal, VI, 69 f., 91.

the tradition, however, is indeterminate. Aishah may have expressed such an opinion at the time that ᶜUmar was trying to put his views across on this matter. Or, again, she may have been led to such a statement later in her life when she watched the foreign slave women "invade" the aristocracy of the Ḥijāz and color the whole moral tone of Islamic society. Neither Aishah nor the rest of the Mothers of the Believers seem to have made any serious protest against ᶜUmar's decision to prohibit them from going on the pilgrimage to Mecca. Yet, there must have been some considerable, but seemingly unrecorded, discontent with this deviation from the practice of Mohammed, for in the last year of his reign ᶜUmar, on the specific request of Mohammed's widows, allowed them to resume the pilgrimage. Zainab had died a few years before, and the aged Sawdah preferred not to go. The rest, veiled and strictly secluded, made the journey as the special charges of ᶜAbd al-Raḥmān ibn ᶜAwf and ᶜUthmān ibn ᶜAffān.[37]

But if Aishah gave no more than silent consent to ᶜUmar's policy in these matters of the mosque and the pilgrimage, she had nothing but praise for the financial provision he made for her and her "sisters." "He sent us," she asserts, "our share of everything, even to the heads and shanks (of slaughtered beasts)."[38] In the matter of income from the confiscated property of the Jews of Khaibar, ᶜUmar gave Moham-

[37] Ibn Saᶜd, VIII, 150 f.; cf. *ibid.*, III[1], 247.

[38] *Ibid.*, III[1], 218; cf. *ibid.*, p. 207.

med's widows choice of payment in land or in produce.[39] When, as a result of the great conquests that brought in tremendous revenues, ᶜUmar, in A.H. 20 (A.D. 641), initiated state pensions, he placed the Mothers of the Believers at the head of the list, allowing each, according to some versions, an annual pension of 12,000 dirhams.[40] According to others, the sums allowed each widow or groups of them differed from Aishah's 12,000 to Ṣafīyah's and Juwairīyah's 5,000 or 6,000 dirhams. The discrimination was based on the status of each wife and her favored position with Mohammed.[41] Those thus discriminated against protested that Mohammed himself had made no distinctions among his wives. ᶜUmar then allowed each widow the sum of 10,000 dirhams, except Aishah, whom he placed first with the sum of 12,000 in recognition of her having been the best beloved of Mohammed.[42] According to some, Aishah refused to accept the extra 2,000;[43] but ᶜUmar must have insisted on it, since later one of her complaints against ᶜUthmān was the reduction of her pension to the figure allowed the rest of Mohammed's widows.[44] Aishah,

[39] Balādhurī, *Futūḥ*, p. 28; cf. Caetani, *op. cit.*, IV, 362 f.

[40] Ibn Saᶜd, III[1], 213, 216; Balādhurī, *Futūḥ*, p. 451; cf. Caetani, *op. cit.*, IV, 388 ff.

[41] Yaᶜqūbī, *Tārīkh*, ed. Houtsma (2 vols.; Lugduni Batavorum, 1883), II, 175; Ibn Saᶜd, III[1], 219; Balādhurī, *Futūḥ*, pp. 454 f.

[42] Ṭabarī, I, 2413; cf. Balādhurī, *Futūḥ*, pp. 449, 454; Ibn Saᶜd, III[1], 119.

[43] Ṭabarī, I, 2413; Ibn al-Athīr, II, 392.

[44] Yaᶜqūbī, II, 203 f.

thus flattered and honored, would hardly be inclined to question ᶜUmar's expenditures from the treasury for his family and self at this stage, though she seems to have been so inclined at the beginning of his reign.[45]

It is clear from the preceding that ᶜUmar was conscious of Aishah's great prestige resulting from the fact of her having been Mohammed's best beloved and of being Abū Bakr's most distinguished and able child. His avowed loyalty to Mohammed and Abū Bakr, together with Aishah's friendly attitude toward his administration, led him to confirm her unique position by placing her first in the state pension system, ahead of all the believers and of the Mothers of the Believers, including even his own daughter Ḥafṣah. The public could have hardly failed to note the cordial relationship existing between the caliph and *the* Mother of the Believers. Perhaps they even sensed Aishah's tacit approval of ᶜUmar's energetic and essentially just management of the affairs of the new state. This may or may not have been the reason why several of the foremost leaders went not to Aishah but to Ḥafṣah when they sought to induce ᶜUmar to relax somewhat his general severity toward the people.[46] It is certain that, when ᶜUmar had passed on, Aishah did not hesitate to pay him frequent and glowing tribute. "He was, by Allah," she would say, "a good manager and an only one of his kind; he was equal to every occasion."[47] Neither did

[45] Ibn Saᶜd, III[1], 222.

[46] *Ibid.*, pp. 199, 222; cf. *ibid.*, pp. 197, 206.

[47] ᶜ*Iqd*, I, 18.

she hesitate to hold up the departed ᶜUmar as a model. Chancing to pass by an inert or sort of a half-dead fellow, she asked disapprovingly who or what he was. On being told he was a Qurʾān reader, she quickly remarked, "ᶜUmar too was a Qurʾān reader, but when he read or spoke, he made one hear; when he walked, he was brisk and quick of step; and when he struck, he hurt."[48] That is, ᶜUmar, in so far as he was not a man of half-measures, was a man after Aishah's own heart.

Aishah's continuing general prestige did not depend solely on ᶜUmar's good will or actions. There are indications that she made it her business to keep informed and be abreast of the times. Though she did not go on any campaigns of the reigns of Abū Bakr and ᶜUmar, yet she must have taken a keen interest in their progress. One finds her, for instance, recounting some of the details of the Battle of Qādisīyah.[49] Neither was she slow to capitalize on her reputation as Mohammed's favorite wife. For it was as such that she claimed, or others tacitly conceded her, intimate knowledge of Mohammed's ways, words, and character. And already in the reign of ᶜUmar, if not indeed in that of Abū Bakr, as some would have it, she had begun to be consulted on such matters as the prophet's *sunnah* or practice and had ventured to give *fatwa*'s or decisions on sacred law or custom.[50]

[48] Mubarrad, *Kāmil*, ed. W. Wright (Leipzig, 1864), p. 325; cf. Ibn Saᶜd, III¹, 208.

[49] Ṭabarī, I, 2251, 2429.

[50] Ibn Saᶜd, II², 126.

Zainab and Umm Salamah, Aishah's closest rivals for the affections of Mohammed, were in line to share in Aishah's prominence in this matter of traditions. But Zainab died early (20/641),[51] and Umm Salamah, though far ahead of the rest of Mohammed's widows, was to prove a poor second to Aishah.

It is difficult to get at details of personal relationships between Aishah and her "sisters" in this period. We read of no stormy scenes stirred up by the Mothers of the Believers now that Mohammed, the main object of their jealousy, was no more. We hear of no challenge to Aishah's favored position financially or otherwise. In matters of public conduct and policy, Mohammed's widows generally behaved and were treated as a unit, being referred to collectively as the "wives of the prophet" or the "Mothers of the Believers." Though those that had families and relatives doubtless went visiting, the group for the most time lived in the mosque apartments. They must, therefore, have seen quite a bit of one another. A few incidents associated with Zainab and her death would seem to indicate that the "Mothers" lived amicably, Mohammed's memory tending to draw them together as his presence had tended to pull them apart.

Mohammed, says Aishah, had told his wives that she of the longest hand or reach would be the first to follow him to the next world. She then relates how after Mohammed's death, whenever they got to-

[51] *Ibid.*, VIII, 81, 78.

gether in the apartment of any one of them, they stood against the wall and measured the reach of their hands to determine which of Mohammed's widows would be the first to depart this world. This they continued to do until Zainab's death settled the question, but not without giving the rest of the "Mothers" some food for thought. For Zainab was short, and her reach was not the longest. But Zainab, it seems, was extremely charitable, and so her "sisters" concluded that, by "the longest of hand," Mohammed had meant the most liberal hand in the cause of charity. Zainab's departure gave them the opportunity to dwell on her charity and on her other admirable qualities of industry, piety, and kindliness to the needy. Aishah, remembering Zainab's generous words on her behalf at the time of the scandal, was foremost in praising and blessing her now departed rival, whose entry into Mohammed's harem had caused so much concern to her and to the new Moslem community.[52]

All in all, though the reigns of Abū Bakr and ᶜUmar afforded Aishah little opportunity to exercise any personal power in the conduct of public and political affairs, they were nevertheless conducive to the enhancement of her personal prestige. ᶜUmar's last acts further sustained that prestige. Fatally wounded by the assassin's knife, ᶜUmar in his last days was much concerned about his own final resting-place and about

[52] *Ibid.*, pp. 37, 78–81; Abū Nuᶜaim, *Ḥilyat al-Awlīyā* . . . . (10 vols.; Cairo, 1932–38), II, 53 f.; *Iṣābah*, IV, 600; Nawawī, p. 842; cf. above, pp. 16–19, 26, 32 f.

the choice of his successor. Anxious though he was to be buried beside his friends, Mohammed and Abū Bakr, whose tombs occupied a section of Aishah's apartment, ᶜUmar would not force Aishah's hand in this matter, but instead asked it of her as a great favor. That he was not any too sure of her favorable response would seem to be indicated by his specific desire to be buried in the Moslem cemetery should Aishah see fit to refuse his request. Though Aishah had thought of saving the space for her own tomb, she now willingly relinquished it in the dying caliph's favor.[53] The small and humble apartment thus came to house the living Aishah and the dead Mohammed, Abū Bakr, and ᶜUmar. And Aishah was conscious, at first at least, not only of the mortal remains but also of the spirits of these men. She felt at home, she tells us, as long as only her husband and father shared her apartment; but, when ᶜUmar came to keep them company, she felt she was in the presence of a stranger. Thereafter she had a wall partition built between the tombs and her own section of the apartment.[54]

ᶜUmar's last major political act was the appointment of an elective council of six to chose his successor from among its members. The six, all first-generation Companions, were, furthermore, among the ten who had won Mohammed's complete and unconditional approval. They were: ᶜUthmān, ᶜAlī, Ṭalḥah,

[53] Ibn Saᶜd, III[1], 245; Bukhārī, II, 433; Ṭabarī, I, 2131, 2725; Nawawī, pp. 495 f.

[54] Ibn Saᶜd, III[1], 264.

Zubair, Saᶜd ibn Abī Waqqāṣ, and ᶜAbd al-Raḥmān ibn ᶜAwf. They were to meet in secret session and make their choice within three days.[55] It is not certain where ᶜUmar wished them to meet. According to some, he had instructed them to meet in *a* house or in the house of one of their members.[56] But, according to others, he wished them to meet in a place close to Aishah's house (probably the treasury).[57] According to still others, he specified Aishah's own apartment as the council's meeting place, provided she gave her consent.[58]

Equal uncertainty prevails as to where the council did actually meet. Some have it in the house of Miswar ibn Makhramah; others, in the house of ᶜAbd al-Raḥmān ibn ᶜAwf, the chairman of the council; and still others place it in the *dār al-māl*, or treasury.[59] But again there are those who believed the meeting actually took place in Aishah's own apartment.[60] In that case ᶜUmar gave a final boost to Aishah's mounting prestige; that and no more. For, regardless of the

55 *Ibid.*, p. 245; Balādhurī, *Ansāb*, V, 16, 18; Ṭabarī, I, 2778. It is doubtful if this council was as official or exclusive as these traditions make it out to be (cf. Caetani, *op. cit.*, V, 82–89).

56 Ibn Saᶜd, III¹, 265; Balādhurī, *Ansāb*, V, 16; Ṭabarī, I, 2779; Ibn al-Athīr, III, 52.

57 Ṭabarī, I, 2778; cf. Muir, *The Caliphate . . . .*, ed. Weir (Edinburgh, 1915), p. 194.

58 ᶜ*Iqd*, II, 257; Ṭabarī, I, 2778; Ibn al-Athīr, III, 51.

59 Balādhurī, *Ansāb*, V, 20 f.; Ṭabarī, I, 2781, 7888; Ibn al-Athīr, III, 53.

60 ᶜ*Iqd*, II, 258; Ṭabarī, I, 2781; Ibn al-Athīr, III, 53.

meeting place, Aishah herself is nowhere credited, officially or otherwise, with any role whatsoever in the deliberations and final choice of the council. In the meantime Aishah's full brother, ᶜAbd al-Raḥmān, took it upon himself to do some detective work and to track down some of the (supposed?) plotters of ᶜUmar's assassination. These, taken by surprise, fled and, in their confusion, dropped a double-pointed dagger which ᶜAbd al-Raḥmān secured and which was later used as proof of their guilt.[61] Such actions emphasize the cordiality that existed between ᶜUmar and the children of Abū Bakr.

That Aishah was keenly interested in the deliberations of the council and had her own preferences as to the candidates is hardly to be doubted. Zubair and Ṭalḥah were closely related to her by ties of blood and marriage. The former was her brother-in-law and father of her "son," ᶜAbd Allah. The latter was her cousin and one-time would-be suitor if she were free to remarry,[62] but probably now the husband of her young sister, Umm Kulthūm, whom ᶜUmar had failed to secure. The election of either of them to the caliphate would have been of immense advantage to the clan of Abū Bakr, for whose welfare Aishah was always on the lookout. Yet, there is no record that she took any steps, at this point, to further their cause. Given a choice between ᶜAlī and ᶜUthmān, she would

[61] Ṭabarī, I, 2797; Ibn Saᶜd, III[1], 258; cf. Caetani, *op. cit.*, V, 94; Della Vida, in *EI*, III, 984.

[62] See above, p. 58.

have undoubtedly preferred the latter, for resentment still stirred in her heart against the ungallant role that ᶜAlī had played in the affair of the slander. Furthermore, she had reason to be better impressed with ᶜUthmān and even to be grateful to him, for Mohammed himself was known to have shown more deference to ᶜUthmān than to either Abū Bakr or ᶜUmar. Aishah was once led to ask Mohammed why he was so particular and so socially proper in the presence of ᶜUthmān. The answer implied that ᶜUthmān himself was so much the gentleman that a casual reception would tend to turn him away without his revealing the object of his visit. Later glorifiers of ᶜUthmān give Mohammed's answer thus: "And why should I not show deference to one whom even the angels respect?"[63]

But Mohammed's courtesy to ᶜUthmān was not altogether a question of good manners. It had a practical side. ᶜUthmān's early conversion, his honored position as an aristocratic Umayyad, and his great wealth which he did not stint in the early service of Islam made him not only a worthy recipient of Mohammed's courtesy but deserving also of his gratitude. His generosity ran the wide range from equipping an expedition to provisioning the impoverished prophet's household.[64] ᶜUthmān's naturally aristocratic bearing did indeed savor of arrogance to those of humbler origins, especially if they had reason to

[63] Ibn Ḥanbal, VI, 62, 155, 167, 288; Balādhurī, *Ansāb*, V, 10.

[64] E.g., Balādhurī, *Ansāb*, V, 8, 10.

view him as a dangerous rival. This is very well brought out in an incident that took place soon after Abū Bakr's election and one that is reported by ʿUthmān himself. ʿUthmān, it seems, failed to return ʿUmar's salutation. ʿUmar reported the insult to Abū Bakr, who, taking him by the hand, confronted ʿUthmān and asked him for an explanation. ʿUthmān denied that he had ignored ʿUmar's greeting. "Yes, by Allah, you did," put in ʿUmar. "It is indeed your haughtiness, O children of Umayyah!" ʿUthmān succeeded in convincing Abū Bakr that, being deeply engrossed with thoughts on the recent death of Allah's Messenger and the future salvation of his people, he had been unaware of ʿUmar's passing-by and of his salutation.[65] Abū Bakr retained ʿUthmān's dignified friendship to the end of his short reign, when ʿUthmān is found to be very helpful and accommodating during the caliph's illness.[66] Such, then, are some of the personal reasons why Aishah would prefer the election of ʿUthmān to that of ʿAli.

It is a well-known fact of Islamic history that ʿUthmān (23–35/644–56) lost no time in advancing the interests of the already powerful Umayyads. The most lucrative and the most important positions at the disposal of the caliph were usually given to his immediate relatives or to others of his clansmen, who in turn seized this opportunity to feather their political nests. Criticism of ʿUthmān's flagrant nepotism was soon in the air. It slowly gathered momentum as

[65] Ibn Saʿd, II², 84 f.

[66] *Ibid.*, III¹, 143.

the first six years or so of his reign passed and as the caliph and his Umayyads showed no signs of mending their ways.[67] In these first years one hears little of any direct dealing between Aishah and ᶜUthmān. She, together with her aristocratic "sisters" of the Makhzūm and Umayyah—Umm Salamah, Maimūnah, and Umm Ḥabībah—approached the new caliph for permission to go on the pilgrimage. Since ᶜUmar had relented and had allowed them to resume the pilgrimage, ᶜUthmān decided to grant their request and graciously to accompany in person any of Mohammed's widows who wished to make the pilgrimage.[68]

But if Aishah had cause to be reasonably satisfied with ᶜUthmān's election and to be somewhat optimistic as to the nature of his rule, she, like a great many of the leaders of the community, soon became aware of his weakness and favoritism. She was to seize upon these as her entering wedge into the field of high politics. ᶜUthmān, some say, saw fit to reduce her pension to the level of the rest of Mohammed's widows.[69] Aishah was not one to overlook such a blow to her unique and privileged position. This, therefore, could have been a likely factor in her eventual and outspoken opposition to his administration. But, even at that, it would have to be but one among many factors. For ᶜUthmān laid himself wide open to criti-

67 Balādhurī, *Ansāb*, V, 25 f.

68 Ibn Saᶜd, III¹, 151.

69 Yaᶜqūbī, II, 203 f.; cf. Wellhausen, *Skizzen und Vorarbeiten*, VI (Berlin, 1899), 126, n. 2.

cism on various scores and from different sources, so much so that even ᶜAbd al-Raḥmān ibn ᶜAwf, his best friend and staunchest supporter and the one man really responsible for his election to the caliphate, came in time to regret the part he had played in that election. Once when ᶜUthmān took seriously ill, he had a deed of succession drawn up by his secretary, who was told to leave vacant space for the insertion of the appointee's name. Then with his own hand ᶜUthmān wrote the name of ᶜAbd al-Raḥmān ibn ᶜAwf, tied up the deed, and sent it by his freedman, Ḥamrān ibn Abān, to Umm Ḥabībah, daughter of Abū Sufyān and Umayyad widow of Mohammed, for secret safekeeping. But Ḥamrān proved untrustworthy, as he did later on another occasion;[70] for he read the deed on the way and took it instead to ᶜAbd al-Raḥmān himself, whose reaction is thus reported: "What," he cried angrily, "I appoint him openly and he appoints me in secret!" The news of the affair spread, and the Umayyads were aroused. Ḥamrān, for his faithlessness, received a hundred strokes and was sent away to Baṣrah. The relationship between ᶜUthmān and ᶜAbd al-Raḥmān was strained to the point of unpleasant comparisons.[71]

Again, as ᶜUthmān's nepotism became apparent, the people said to ᶜAbd al-Raḥmān, "This is all your doing!" Unable to escape the accusation and its implied guilt, ᶜAbd al-Raḥmān answered, "I did not think him capable of it. I swear to Allah I will not

[70] Balādhurī, *Ansāb*, V, 57 f.

[71] Yaᶜqūbī, II, 195 f.

speak to him ever!" And ᶜAbd al-Raḥmān was as good as his word, for when ᶜUthmān visited him on his deathbed in 32 (A.D. 652–53), ᶜAbd al-Raḥmān turned his face to the wall and would not speak to the caliph. He further left instructions that ᶜUthmān was not to pray over his body.[72] Aishah and Umm Salamah, by far the most active of the Mothers of the Believers, had nothing but warm gratitude and glowing praise for ᶜAbd al-Raḥmān because of his great consideration and liberal generosity to them and to others.[73] They, therefore, could hardly have failed to see matters his way.

But ᶜUthmān, in his treatment of another Companion of the prophet, ᶜAmmār ibn Yāsir,[74] gave both women an excellent opportunity for open opposition. ᶜAmmār was Umm Salamah's uterine brother. His character and honesty of purpose is said to have been witnessed to by Aishah herself on the grounds that she had heard Mohammed speak highly of him.[75] ᶜUmar had appointed him to the governorship of Kūfah, but he was not strong or stern enough to retain the office for long.[76] He was, however, courageous enough to challenge ᶜUthmān's misuse of the resources of the

72 Balādhurī, *Ansāb*, V, 57; Abū al-Fidā, *Annals* (Hafniae, 1789–94), I, 258.

73 Ibn Ḥanbal, VI, 135, 307, 317; Ibn al-Jauzī, *Ṣifat al-Ṣafwah* (4 vols.; Haidarābād, 1936–37), I, 136 f.

74 Ibn Saᶜd, III¹, 176–89, VIII, 63; *Ansāb*, V, 48–52.

75 Ibn Ḥanbal, VI, 113; Tirmidhī, XIII, 208, 259; Nawawī, p. 487.

76 Balādhurī, *Futūḥ*, p. 279.

Moslems, which on this particular occasion took the form of misappropriating some jewels from the treasury. For his daring courage ᶜAmmār was publicly flogged until he was unconscious, and it was in that condition that he was carried into the house of his sister, Umm Salamah. The Makhzūmite Hishām ibn al-Walīd, brother of the more famous Khālid ibn al-Walīd, protested ᶜUthmān's high-handedness and was himself insulted. He too reported to Umm Salamah, in whose house other Makhzūmites gathered. ᶜUthmān sent to ask her, "What means this gathering?" Her message came back, "Put aside this (conduct) from you, O ᶜUthmān, and do not by your order force on the people that which they abhor."[77] When Aishah heard of ᶜUthmān's treatment of ᶜAmmār, she was extremely angry. She took one of Mohammed's hairs, a shirt, and a sandal of his and, holding them for all to see, exclaimed, "How soon indeed you have forgotten the practice (*sunnah*) of your prophet, and these, his hair, shirt, and sandal have not yet perished!" ᶜUthmān, angered to the point of speechlessness, was nevertheless outmaneuvered and had to take refuge for the time being in the mosque. So impressed and astounded were the people at the turn of affairs that they could say or do nothing but marvel and praise Allah. ᶜAmr ibn al-ᶜĀṣ, himself a victim of ᶜUthmān's nepotism—for the latter had ousted him from the governorship of Egypt in favor of his half-brother, ᶜAbd Allah ibn Saᶜd, better known as Ibn Abī

[77] Balādhurī, *Ansāb*, V, 48 f.

Sarḥ—marveled and praised Allah the loudest.[78] Aishah had now openly joined the opposition. She had also discovered an effective propaganda tool in the use of Mohammed's relics.[79]

Provincial affairs gave Aishah her opportunity to play her hand against ᶜUthmān. The latter, early in his reign, had been forced by public pressure to recall his governor of Kūfah, Saᶜd ibn Abī Waqqāṣ, for his refusal to repay into the Kūfan treasury a sum of money advanced him by the low-born but strict treasurer, ᶜAbd Allah ibn Masᶜūd. ᶜUthmān replaced Saᶜd in that turbulent city's governorship by his (ᶜUthmān's) uterine brother Walīd ibn ᶜUqbah (25–30/644–650/51), who, though he retained Ibn Masᶜūd as treasurer, tried, nevertheless, to misuse the treasury. Ibn Masᶜūd would not oblige. Walīd complained to ᶜUthmān, who reminded Ibn Masᶜūd that he was *their* treasurer and that he was, therefore, *not* to oppose Walīd. The indignant Ibn Masᶜūd threw down the keys of the treasury with the retort, "I thought I was a treasurer for the Moslems; but if I am a treasurer for you, then I have no need of that (office)."[80] He remained, however, in Kūfah but definitely in the ranks of the opposition and a thorn, therefore, in the side of Walīd. When ᶜUthmān, in his effort to issue a

[78] *Ibid.*, pp. 48 f., 88 f.

[79] Even in the Arab world of today, relics of the beloved dead are cherished for long years and displayed on many an occasion of private and ceremonial mourning.

[80] Balādhurī, *Ansāb*, V, 30 f.

standard text of the Qurʾān, ordered all other texts destroyed, Ibn Masᶜūd refused to yield his. This, together with Walīd's persistent complaints of his disturbing influence in Kūfah, led ᶜUthmān to order Ibn Masᶜūd to Medina. Arrived in the city, he went to the mosque where the caliph was making a speech. Soon the two came to sharp words, with Aishah taking ᶜUthmān to task for his rough speech to a Companion of the Messenger of Allah. This probably enraged ᶜUthmān all the more. At any rate, he ordered Ibn Masᶜūd thrown out of the mosque. His order was carried out with such violence that among the physical injuries suffered by Ibn Masᶜūd were two broken ribs. It was then that Aishah let go of herself and spoke out her mind freely, or as the historian reports with tantalizing brevity, "And then Aishah spoke and she said plenty."[81] Ibn Masᶜūd was thereafter forbidden to leave Medina lest he cause trouble wherever he went. He was, besides, subjected to financial deprivations. Just before his death (A.H. 32 or 33) ᶜUthmān attempted a reconciliation; but Ibn Masᶜūd said he had no need now of the caliph's favors. Like ᶜAbd al-Raḥmān ibn ᶜAwf, he too left word that ᶜUthmān was not to pray over his body—a service which was performed, some say, by ᶜAmmār ibn Yāsir.[82]

In the meantime, matters at Kūfah had not gone any too well for Walīd ibn ᶜUqbah, whose fondness

[81] Yaᶜqūbī, II, 196 f.; Balādhurī, *Ansāb*, V, 36 f.

[82] Yaᶜqūbī, II, 197 f.; Balādhurī, *Ansāb*, V, 37; but cf. Ibn Saᶜd, III[1], 113; Ṭabarī, I, 2894; Nawawī, pp. 371 f.

for his cups was soon to prove his undoing. ʿUthmān had repeatedly turned a deaf ear to complaints against his intemperance on the pretext of demanding proof and witnesses. Both were eventually found by the determined opposition. The proof came in the form of Walīd's official signet ring, which they slipped off his finger while he lay in drunken sleep. Finally, men were found who were willing to testify that Walīd had misconducted public prayers while drunk. The opposition, with its proof and witnesses, arrived at Medina and this time confidently sought out the caliph. But ʿUthmān still balked. He scolded the witnesses and dismissed the group. They went to Aishah, who now accused ʿUthmān of "withholding punishment and intimidating witnesses." Again the two came to sharp words, while the crowds meanwhile gathered in the mosque. Exasperated, ʿUthmān demanded of Aishah, "What have you to do with this? You were ordered to stay at home." This raised a new issue: did Aishah (and therefore women in general) have or have not the right to speak and take action in matters of public affairs? Moslem opinion divided then and there on the question. Some sided with ʿUthmān, but others demanded to know who indeed had a better right than Aishah in such matters. Words flew back and forth until a free-for-all fight developed with the ready-to-hand sandals for weapons. The crowd was in time quieted down, but the scandal had reached such proportions that ʿUthmān was forced to depose his brother and to subject him to the legal punishment for drunkenness—a public flogging.[83]

ᶜUthmān now appointed as his governor of Kūfah another kinsman, Saᶜīd ibn al-ᶜĀṣ (30–34/650/51–654/55), who was to have no smoother sailing with the stormy Kūfans than had his predecessor. He fell out with Hishām ibn ᶜUtbah over the exact moment of breaking the fast of Ramaḍān and appeased his wrath by ordering Hishām beaten and his house burned. Hishām's sister and some of his friends brought the matter to ᶜUthmān's attention. The caliph, perhaps not expecting his words to be taken seriously, said to them, "Beat Saᶜīd as he beat Hishām, and burn his house as he burned Hishām's house." Soon a fire was set to Saᶜīd's house in Medina. The news reached Aishah in time for her to plead with the party to desist, and her request was honored.[84]

Meanwhile the inexperienced and haughty Saᶜīd was making more dangerous enemies in Kūfah, among them the restless and able leader Mālik ibn al-Ḥārith, better known as al-Ashtar. Saᶜīd succeeded in securing an order from ᶜUthmān to send these trouble-makers off to Syria, whence presently came Muᶜāwiyah's complaint that he did not relish these trouble-makers any more than did Saᶜīd. According to some accounts, ᶜUthmān ordered them back to Kūfah. Presently Ashtar headed a delegation to

[83] Balādhurī, *Ansāb*, V, 33–35; *Aghānī*, IV, 180 f.; Ṭabarī, I, 2840–49.

[84] Ibn Saᶜd, V, 21.

ᶜUthmān, demanding Saᶜīd's dismissal. It happened that Saᶜīd himself was at Medina at the time. ᶜUthmān refused to take any action against Saᶜīd, whereupon Ashtar hastened ahead of Saᶜīd to Kūfah and took possession of the government in defiance of ᶜUthmān. He sent back word to Medina, demanding that ᶜUthmān confirm his candidates for office—Abū Mūsā al-Ashᶜarī and Ḥudhaifah ibn al-Yamān—insolently adding, "and keep away from us your Walīd and your Saᶜīd, and any of your kinsmen you may fancy."[85] Again ᶜUthmān had to yield.[86] What part, if any, Aishah played in this new development does not seem to be recorded. It is perhaps worthy of note here that her brother, ᶜAbd al-Raḥmān, was one of ᶜUthmān's two messengers that carried a letter to Ashtar calling that rebel back to obedience.[87]

Troubles were likewise stirring in the provinces of Egypt, where the events involved Aishah's younger and half-brother, Mohammed, the son of Abū Bakr and Asmā bint ᶜUmais. Mohammed, born in the Year 10 (A.D. 632), was but a child at the time of his father's death and the object, therefore, of Aishah's care and affection. His mother was the widow of Jaᶜfar ibn Abī Ṭālib at the time of her marriage to Abū Bakr, and after the latter's death she married her brother-in-law, ᶜAlī ibn Abī Ṭālib. She bore sons

[85] Balādhurī, *Ansāb*, V, 46.

[86] Ibn Saᶜd, V, 21–23; Balādhurī, *Ansāb*, V, 39–47; Ṭabarī, I, 2907–20, 2927–31.

[87] Balādhurī, *Ansāb*, V, 46.

to all three of her husbands.[88] In all probability Mohammed, being still a child, accompanied his mother into the household of his stepfather ʿAlī, grew up with his other half-brothers and sisters, and thus came to look upon himself as a member of ʿAlī's family. A family scene is recorded in which the different half-brothers indulged in lively braggadocio about the comparative merits of their respective fathers. Asmā and ʿAlī had to intervene to keep the peace, with ʿAlī calling on Asmā for the deciding word. "I have not seen an Arab youth that was better than Jaʿfar or a mature man that was better than Abū Bakr," she answered.

"You have left nothing for us," said ʿAlī.

"By Allah," came back her answer, "of the three you are the least choice."

"Had you said otherwise," answered the self-effacing ʿAlī, "I would have detested you!"[89] This common family life would explain in part, at least, Mohammed's constant adherence to ʿAlī and his cause. Asmā's own inclinations were probably with the *ahl al-bait*, that is, the People of the House, as Mohammed's family, including both the ʿAbbāsid and the ʿAlīd branches, came to be called; for she and several of her sisters were allied by marriage with the prophet's family. Among these were her half-sister, Maimūnah, Mohammed's wife, and Umm al-Faḍl,

[88] Ibn Saʿd, III[1], 119 f., 145; IV[1], 23; Ṭabarī, I, 2130; *Iṣābah*, IV, 438 f.

[89] Ibn Saʿd, IV[1], 28; *Iṣābah*, IV, 439.

wife of ʿAbbās.[90] Mohammed, therefore, may have been influenced by his mother in favor of the ʿAlīd-ʿAbbāsid interests. Be that as it may, this youthful brother, as yet only in his early twenties, went much further than Aishah in his opposition to ʿUthmān, and later fought on the side of ʿAlī and against sister Aishah in the Battle of the Camel. ʿAlī later mourned his death like that of a real son.

The political career of this, the most ambitious of Abū Bakr's sons, was stormy and brief. He first comes on the political scene in Egypt and seemingly from the start in the company of Mohammed ibn Abī Ḥudhaifah. The situation in Egypt was in many respects parallel to that in ʿIrāq. The man who had replaced the conqueror of Egypt, ʿAmr ibn al-ʿĀṣ, in the rich governorship of that province was Ibn Abī Sarḥ (25–35/644–56), who, like Walīd of Kūfah, was a uterine brother of ʿUthmān. The opposition party denounced his administration because it was openly run in the interests of the house of ʿUthmān and because it made possible the diversion into private Umayyad pockets of great wealth both from the revenue of Egypt and from the spoils of war in the conquest of the territories to the west. Marwān ibn al-Ḥakam, for instance, received a fifth of the returns from Africa.[91] Ibn Abī Sarḥ's preoccupation with these same conquests, to the neglect of Egyptian affairs, was seized upon as another cause of complaint. Moham-

[90] E.g., Nawawī, p. 825.

[91] E.g., Balādhurī, *Ansāb*, V, 25, 27 f., 38, 52, 88.

med ibn Abī Ḥudhaifah, though he had been brought up by ᶜUthmān, nursed a personal grudge against that caliph, and would brook no restraint or command from Ibn Abī Sarḥ, whom he frequently startled and annoyed with his booming voice raised in prayer. When Ibn Abī Sarḥ refused to take him on the naval expedition of 34 (A.D. 655) against the Byzantines, he retorted, "We go not with you but with the Moslems." He then went sailing either alone, or, as some have it, accompanied by Mohammed ibn Abī Bakr, in a ship manned by or carrying only Copts. In vain did Ibn Abī Sarḥ seek to get rid of the two Mohammeds. For though he pointed out to ᶜUthmān that they were sowing discord and were not to be trusted in the campaigns, ᶜUthmān refused to take action against them or recall them from Egypt. "As for Mohammed ibn Abī Bakr," he wrote, "I credit him to Abū Bakr and to Aishah the Mother of the Believers. And as for Mohammed ibn Abī Ḥudhaifah, he is my son and the son of my brother; I have brought him up and he is the fledgeling of the Quraish."[92]

ᶜUthmān tried to win over his "son" with large gifts, but the latter made this move public and accused the caliph of trying to bribe him away from his duty as a good Moslem. ᶜUthmān next made his peace with ᶜAmmār ibn Yāsir and sent him to Egypt

[92] *Ibid.*, pp. 49–51; Ṭabarī, I, 2869–71; Ibn Taghrībirdī, *Nujūm* .... ("Annals"), ed. W. Popper (Berkeley, Calif., 1909——), I, 69 f.; cf. Caetani, *op. cit.*, VIII, 95 ff.

to look into the affair of Ibn Abī Ḥudhaifah. ʿAmmār went, but instead of easing matters for ʿUthmān he strengthened the cause of Mohammed.[93] He returned later to Medina only to strengthen further the cause of the discontents, who in the next year (35/656) poured into the capital city of Medina from all the major provinces except Syria, demanding redress and change of governors. The candidate for governor of Egypt was Mohammed ibn Abī Bakr, who accompanied the Egyptian force to Medina, while his friend, Mohammed ibn Abī Ḥudhaifah, stayed in the Egyptian capital of Fusṭāṭ. When Ibn Abī Sarḥ pursued the departing Egyptians, Mohammed ibn Abī Ḥudhaifah broke out in open rebellion, seized the government in his absence, and on his return forced him to take flight into Palestine.[94] The rebel now did all he could to keep the resentment of the Egyptians burning against ʿUthmān. He even resorted to forging letters effectively in the name of the Mothers of the Believers. The plural here is significant; for it will be remembered that Aishah and Umm Salamah were half-sisters to Mohammed ibn Abī Bakr and ʿAmmār, respectively, and that they were both known to be in opposition to the caliph. The burden of these letters was, in effect, an appeal to Allah and to the Egyptians for deliverance from the evil rule of ʿUth-

[93] Balādhurī, *Ansāb*, V, 51; Ṭabarī, I, 2943 f., 2961.

[94] Balādhurī, *Ansāb*, V, 61, 67; Ṭabarī, I, 2999; Ibn Taghrībirdī, I, 91, 105 f.

mān.[95] Mohammed ibn Abī Ḥudhaifah held his own in Egypt until after the murder of ᶜUthmān and the Battle of the Camel, when Muᶜāwiyah and his Syrians invaded Egypt and forced him into a truce which was not kept. He and some of his companions were imprisoned. They escaped but were overtaken and slain in 36 (A.D. 657).[96]

In the meanwhile the rebels gathered in Medina had grown bolder in their demands and angrier in their denunciation. Their position was strengthened by the lack of any genuine support for the caliph and by the absence of any united Medinan or Ḥijāzian party. In fact, the City of the Prophet swarmed with notables, the foremost of whom, though seemingly working together at times, were in reality striving to forward their own political ambitions. ᶜAlī, Ṭalḥah, and Zubair had been rival candidates for the caliphate at the time of ᶜUthmān's election. The first two had taken the oath of allegiance reluctantly and under some pressure from the caliph-maker, ᶜAbd al-Raḥmān ibn ᶜAwf. They were personally ambitious and represented also the hopes and ambitions of their family, clans, and supporters. The caliph's own Umayyads seem to have been unprepared for such a major crisis, while his cousin and secretary, Marwān

[95] Kindī, *Kitāb al-Wulāh wa-Kitāb al-Quḍah* ("Governors and Judges of Egypt"), ed. R. Guest (Leiden and London, 1912), pp. 14 f.; cf. also Balādhurī, *Ansāb*, V, 103; Maqrīzī, *Khiṭṭaṭ* (Cairo, 1270/1853), II, 335.

[96] Ṭabarī, I, 3233; Ibn Taghrībirdī, I, 106 f.; cf. Giorgio Levi Della Vida, "Il Califato di Ali secondo il *Kitāb Ansāb al-Aśrāf* di al-Balāḏurī," *Rivista degli studi orientali*, VI (1913–15), 498.

ibn al-Ḥakam, either miscounseled or, as some believe, deliberately double-crossed him. The aged and perplexed caliph, advised to take a conciliatory attitude by Aishah, ᶜAlī, and the others, was urged by Marwān to show stern resistance to the insurgents. ᶜUthmān in the end yielded and dismissed the provincials with soft words and fair promises. This was too much for Marwān, who nearly undid the good work already accomplished by indulging in rough speeches. ᶜAlī, enraged at Marwān, served notice on ᶜUthmān that he need not expect any further help from him if Marwān's counsel was to prevail. In this ᶜAlī was supported by ᶜUthmān's young and faithful wife, Nāʾilah, who questioned Marwān's sincerity and the wisdom of his advice and actions.[97]

Among some of the points yielded to the Egyptian demands was the appointment of Mohammed ibn Abī Bakr as governor of Egypt.[98] Mohammed and his party, thus pacified, started out for that province. When, but three days' journey from Medina, they saw behind them a rider approaching in great haste, they stopped him to ask his name and mission. The youth claimed he was a servant of the caliph or, according to others, of Marwān. Asked if he carried a message, the boy answered in the negative, but the Egyptians were suspicious. They searched him and found in a secret base to his inkwell a letter stamped

[97] E.g., Balādhurī, *Ansāb*, V, 26, 64 f.; cf. *ibid.*, pp. 61 f., 89, 94; Ṭabarī, I, 2974–77; Ibn al-Athīr, III, 130–32.

[98] Balādhurī, *Ansāb*, V, 26.

with the caliph's seal and addressed to Ibn Abī Sarḥ, instructing the latter to put the leaders of the returning Egyptian party to death. Evidently ʿUthmān was not up to date on Mohammed ibn Abī Ḥudhaifah's progress in Egypt. Be that as it may, Mohammed ibn Abī Bakr and the rest, outraged at the double deal, returned to Medina in an ugly mood and confronted ʿUthmān with the letter and its carrier. Acknowledging his servant and his seal, ʿUthmān nevertheless denied any knowledge of the letter. His enemies were quick to point out that if he wrote the letter he was a rogue and if he wrote it not, then he was a fool at the mercy of rogues. Therefore, they loudly argued, he was, in either case, unfit to rule. ʿUthmān, it seems, suspected ʿAlī or Marwān as the author.[99] The handwriting, it was claimed, was that of Marwān. They, therefore, demanded that Marwān be delivered to them so they could question him in the matter. ʿUthmān refused to submit his kinsman to this sort of treatment.[100] Perhaps he feared for Marwān's life; for even ʿAlī thought that, had Marwān been delivered to the angry crowd, he would have been killed before any legal judgment could have been given in his case.[101]

The demand for ʿUthmān's resignation grew louder and uglier and was presently accompanied by threats of murder. ʿUthmān stood his ground. He would not, he said, referring to the caliphate, take off a robe that

[99] Ṭabarī, I, 2964 f., 2983 f., 2992–97; Balādhurī, *Ansāb*, V, 66.

[100] Balādhurī, *Ansāb*, V, 68 f.

[101] *Ibid.*, p. 70.

Allah himself had clothed him with, neither would he bear arms against the believers. With this stubborn and negative attitude, he allowed himself to be surrounded and besieged in his own house.

What, it is time to ask, was Aishah doing as matters went thus from bad to worse? There seem to be no definite incidents associated with her in the earlier stages of this period, though the statement is frequently met with that she urged and instigated the people against ᶜUthmān and censured him severely; or, again, that she taunted and slandered him with epigrams.[102] She was probably as much, if not more, roused and outraged as the Egyptian leaders had been at the episode of the letter which commanded these leaders' treacherous murder, including that of her own brother Mohammed. She may, therefore, have joined in the demand for ᶜUthmān's abdication, though again no definite statement to that effect is found. That she, and most probably Umm Salamah too, was in the front ranks of the opposition is to be inferred from a number of definite incidents in the later stages of the period under consideration. The besieged caliph, in a desperate effort to save the situation, humbled himself, repented of his deeds, and promised anything and everything short of his abdication. One of his promises was not "to appoint any one as *amīr* or governor except him on whom the wives of the prophet and those of counsel among you have agreed."[103] Again as the siege of several weeks

[102] *Ibid.*, pp. 70, 68.

[103] *Ibid.*, pp. 90, 76; Ṭabarī, I, 3043.

progressed and ᶜUthmān's water supply was cut off, he appealed for aid to ᶜAlī, Ṭalḥah, Zubair, Aishah, and the rest of the widows of the prophet. Of the last group, Ṣafīyah, who had previously defended ᶜUthmān, made an unsuccessful attempt to reach him in person, though she managed to get food and water to him by means of a plank placed between their dwellings.[104] The Umayyad Umm Ḥabībah responded readily but was attacked and roughly handled as she sought to make her way through the crowd to ᶜUthmān's house. Aishah took note of the temper of the crowd that would offer such indignities to a widow of Mohammed.[105]

The insurgents' cry now was for the blood of ᶜUthmān. This must have made Aishah stop and think, for she had no wish to go that far. When, therefore, she was sounded on the question, she definitely refused to sanction any idea of the caliph's murder. The rebel Ashtar, who had had his own way in Kūfah in the previous year, came during the siege to feel her out and to ask, "What do *you* say about killing ᶜUthmān?"

"Allah forbid," she answered, "that I should command the shedding of the blood of the Moslems and the killing of their Imām."

Puzzled, if not disappointed, Ashtar answered, "You (plural) wrote us until now when the (civil) war stands on a footing upon which you placed it, you for-

[104] *EI*, IV, 57; Caetani, *op. cit.*, VIII, 223–36.

[105] Balādhurī, *Ansāb*, V, 77; Ṭabarī, I, 3009–11.

bid us (it)."[106] Aishah was repeatedly to deny having ever written any letters against ᶜUthmān; several traditions assert that letters were forged in her name.[107] The use of the plural here recalls the letters that Mohammed ibn Abī Ḥudhaifah of Egypt forged in the name of the widows of Mohammed. There was, it must be also remembered, considerable co-operation between the conspirators in these two provinces.

It was now time for the annual pilgrimage, and Aishah was preparing for the journey to Mecca. ᶜUthmān, perhaps aware of Aishah's pronouncement against the shedding of his blood, sent Marwān with one or two others to plead with her not to leave the city. Their argument was that Allah might use her and her presence in defense of ᶜUthmān. Her answer is variously given and may imply either that Marwān approached her more than once or, more likely, that his persistent request brought forth several excuses: "Do you desire that I should be subjected to the same treatment that was meted out to Umm Ḥabībah and then find no one to protect me? No, by Allah, I will not be (so) dishonored; and I know not where these people's affair will end";[108] or, "I have taken to my camel and have imposed the pilgrimage on myself, and by Allah I will not do (what you ask)";[109] or,

[106] Balādhurī, *Ansāb*, V, 102; Ibn Saᶜd, VIII, 356. Ashtar later refused to be a party to the murder (cf. Balādhurī, *Ansāb*, V, 81, 92, 96; Ibn Saᶜd, III[1], 50 f.; Ṭabarī, I, 2990; Wellhausen, *op. cit.*, VI, 134; Della Vida, "Il Califato . . . .'," *op. cit.*, pp. 459 f.).

[107] Balādhurī, *Ansāb*, V, 103; Ibn Saᶜd, III[1], 57; *ᶜIqd*, II, 266.

[108] Ṭabarī, I, 3011.

[109] Balādhurī, *Ansāb*, V, 75.

again, "I have sweated (in packing) and have closed my bags and I cannot stay."[110] But Marwān persisted and enraged Aishah by citing the following verse: "And Qais set the country afire against me, and then, when it was ablaze, he ran away."

"O you who quote me poems," she is reported as saying, "would to Allah that you and this your friend who intrusts his affair to you had each a millstone round his foot, and both of you were at the bottom of the sea"; or, what seems to be a variant of the preceding, "O, Marwān, would to Allah that he (ᶜUthmān) were in one of these my sacks, and I were able to carry him and cast him into the sea."[111] In other words, Aishah was anxious to be rid of this whole affair, for she was now in a betwixt and between position. She could not find it in her heart either to defend ᶜUthmān or to go the limit with his enemies. She seems even to have had some doubts as to her ability to restrain the latter. She had but little influence on her own brother Mohammed, who was among the foremost of the Egyptian group and whom she tried in vain to persuade to accompany her on the pilgrimage. Her brother, ᶜAbd al-Raḥmān, likewise remained in the capital city, but little is known of his activities at this particular time. So Aishah fled the troubled

[110] Ibn Saᶜd, V, 25.

[111] *Ibid.;* Balādhurī, *Ansāb,* V, 75; Yāᶜqūbī, II, 204. Caetani (*op. cit.,* VIII, 196 f.) believes these to be Shīᶜite fabrications. Professor Sprengling suggests that the third-person pronoun in these sentences was first used by Aishah to refer not to ᶜUthmān but to the entire troubled situation and that it was this situation she wished to cast to the bottom of the sea.

scenes of Medina alone and with wrath in her heart against both ʿUthmān and the Egyptians.[112]

ʿUthmān had appointed ʿAbd Allah ibn al-ʿAbbās leader of the pilgrimage and had sent messages with him to his Meccan friends and to the pilgrims gathered in the holy city to come to his aid. When the pilgrim procession halted at Ṣulṣul, some seven miles out of Medina, ʿAbd Allah approached Aishah and a conversation took place between them. The gist of this conversation, when its glaring ʿAbbāsid color is removed, would seem to indicate that Aishah expected and approved ʿUthmān's removal from office and hoped for the election of her cousin Ṭalḥah, who, she predicted, would be a good ruler and follow the course taken by Abū Bakr. "O Mother!" said the son of ʿAbbās, "if anything should happen to the man (ʿUthmān), the people will take refuge with none but our friend (ʿAlī)."

"Be silent, you!" she promptly rebuked him. "I want none of your boasts or arguments."[113]

But if Aishah thus forsook ʿUthmān in his hour of greatest need, it must also be pointed out that she at the same time deserted her relatives, Ṭalḥah and Zubair, in what she must have suspected, if not indeed known, to be their hour of greatest opportunity. For it was becoming more and more evident that should ʿUthmān be removed, by means fair or foul, the rivals for the vacant caliphate would be ʿAlī,

[112] Ṭabarī, I, 3010 f.; Ibn al-Athīr, III, 139.

[113] Ṭabarī, I, 3040; Balādhurī, *Ansāb*, V, 75.

Ṭalḥah, and Zubair. Perhaps wishful thinking had helped to convince her that in that eventuality, Ṭalḥah and Zubair, alone or together, would be a match for ᶜAlī. Taken all in all, therefore, Aishah's attitude at this point of the threatening political development and her determined flight to Mecca would seem to indicate a real though belated desire on her part to be rid of so troublesome a situation.

Events in Medina moved with accelerated speed during the next three weeks.[114] The rebels realized that they must act quickly and force matters to a conclusion before effective aid could reach the besieged caliph from Mecca and from Syria; for a desperate cry for help had gone out also to Muᶜāwiyah. ᶜAlī, Ṭalḥah, and Zubair kept aloof from the caliph, though they sent their sons to stand guard at his house.[115] The Egyptians, led by Mohammed ibn Abī Bakr, forced their way into the house, and dispatched the defenseless ᶜUthmān, who preferred to die reading the Qurʾān instead of wielding the sword against the believers. His faithful and courageous wife, Nāʾilah, sought to protect him and was herself wounded in the hand, suffering the loss of some of her fingers.[116] Mohammed went out of his way to insult the aged and unresisting caliph but stopped short of actually shed-

[114] Dīnawarī, *Akhbār al-Ṭiwāl*, ed. Vladimir Guirgass (Leiden, 1888), p. 150.

[115] E.g., Balādhurī, *Ansāb*, V, 78, 79 f.

[116] Ṭabarī, I, 3020, 3255; Balādhurī, *Ansāb*, V, 69–71; Ibn al-Ṭiqṭaqā, *Al-Fakhrī* ("Histoire"), ed. H. Derenbourg (Paris, 1895), p. 137; cf. Abbott, "Women and the State in Early Islam," *JNES*, I (1942), 106–26.

ding his blood. Nāʾilah, though she testified to this fact, did nevertheless hold Mohammed responsible for her husband's murder, arguing that it was he who forced his way in and led the actual murderers to their victim.[117] And she was not alone in thus counting Mohammed ibn Abī Bakr among the real regicides. The murder took place on the eighteenth of the month of Dhū al-Ḥijjah, A.H. 35, that is, June 17, A.D. 656. Within the next day or two ʿUthmān was hurriedly buried at night in secrecy. Aishah's brother, ʿAbd al-Raḥmān, wished to pray over the body but was refused the privilege.[118] In the meantime, some of the Umayyads took to cover, aided by Umm Ḥabībah, who sheltered large groups of them, hiding quite a few in the granary, among other places.[119] Others took to flight, some to Mecca and some to Syria.

The field was now clear for the three rivals, ʿAlī, Ṭalḥah, and Zubair. ʿAlī's party, for once, stole a march on the others, with Ashtar among the first to take the oath of allegiance to ʿAlī.[120] Ṭalḥah and Zubair either went of their own accord to ʿAlī or were called by him for a conference. Many a tradition has it that they were then, with the sword of Ashtar over their heads, forced to take the oath of allegiance to ʿAlī.[121] Some even assert that Zubair never did take

[117] Balādhurī, *Ansāb*, V, 70 f.; cf. Ibn Saʿd, III[1], 51.

[118] Balādhurī, V, 83, 86.

[119] *Ibid.*, p. 80.

[120] Ṭabarī, I, 3075.

[121] *Ibid.*, pp. 3069, 3070–78.

the oath.[122] The two, nevertheless, remained in Medina and, outwardly at least, co-operated with ᶜAlī.

As the weeks passed into months, it became more and more apparent that ᶜAlī had no intentions of punishing the regicides, that as an executive he was weak and vacillating, and that he was little disposed to give office to any but members of his own party. The request of Ṭalḥah and Zubair for the governorships of Baṣrah and Kūfah, which cities were known to favor them, respectively, was refused.[123] They tried on more than one occasion to leave Medina, but ᶜAlī would not permit them. It was, therefore, not until some four months after the murder of ᶜUthmān that the two managed to leave for Mecca under pretext of performing the lesser pilgrimage,[124] but in reality to join the Meccan opposition party already championed by Aishah.[125] To this we now turn our attention.

II

Aishah, though she had insisted on making the pilgrimage, had no other thought than to return to Medina once that pilgrimage was over. Having washed her hands of both parties at Medina, she was out of any significant touch with the rapid march of

[122] *Ibid.*, pp. 3070, 3077.

[123] *Ibid.*, pp. 3060, 3073.

[124] *Ibid.*, pp. 3069, 3091.

[125] *Ibid.*, pp. 3099; cf. Wellhausen, *The Arab Kingdom and Its Fall*, trans. Margaret Graham Weir (Calcutta, 1927), p. 52; Muir, *op. cit.*, pp. 240 f.

events in that city. There is no record of further appeals to her from ʿUthmān and his party or of any attempt on the part of Ṭalḥah and Zubair to keep her informed. Nevertheless, she could not be expected to be indifferent to what was going on in the City of the Prophet. She was now, in fact, eagerly asking for information from newcomers from Medina. The earliest reports were contradictory. One man stated that ʿUthmān had killed the Egyptians. Aishah, amazed, exclaimed, "Does he then kill those who come asking for (their) rights and denouncing injustice? By Allah, we do not approve of this." But presently a second comer reversed the first report and stated that the Egyptians had killed ʿUthmān. Others, fugitives from Medina, confirmed this, adding that no one had agreed to accept the command. "How shrewd indeed!" said Aishah. Then, referring no doubt to the whole perplexing situation, she added, "This is the result of the complaints circulating among you in the cries for reforms."[126] Another account reports her reaction in these words: "I see that ʿUthmān will draw ill-luck upon his people as Abū Sufyān drew ill-luck upon his people in the Battle of Badr,"[127] referring to Mohammed's defeat of the Quraish who were led by Abū Sufyān.

Aishah now made no haste, as did ʿAbd Allah ibn al-ʿAbbās, among others, to return to Medina, for she had yet the *ʿUmrah*, or lesser pilgrimage, to perform. That done, she started on the return trip. At Sarif, a

[126] *Ibid.*, pp. 3096, 3098.

[127] Balādhurī, *Ansāb*, V, 91.

place some six to twelve miles out of Mecca,[128] she met one of her maternal relatives, ᶜUbaid ibn Abī Salimah, who, on being asked for the news, first kept silent and then just mumbled to himself. "A plague on you," cried the impatient Aishah. "Is it against us or for us?"

"The people of Medina agreed on (the election of) ᶜAlī, and the crowd is in control of the city."

"I do not think this affair is ended," said Aishah. Then turning to her group she ordered, "Take me back."[129] An ᶜAlīd version records her first reaction to ᶜUthmān's murder in a phrase that can be freely translated as "Curse him!" and gives her comment on the entire situation, including ᶜAlī's election, in a sentence, again freely translated as, "I did not think matters would take this course."[130]

Arrived once again at Mecca, she was met by ᶜUthmān's governor of that city, ᶜAbd Allah ibn ᶜĀmir al-Ḥaḍramī, who asked, "What brings you back, O Mother of the Believers?"

"The fact that ᶜUthmān was killed unjustly, and that order will not be re-established so long as this rabble has command. Demand revenge for the blood of ᶜUthmān and so restore and strengthen Islam!" She went to the mosque and took her stand at the

[128] Yāqūt, *Muᶜjam al-Buldān (Geog. Dict.)*, ed. Wüstenfeld (6 vols., Leipzig, 1924).

[129] Ṭabarī, I, 3096–98.

[130] Yaᶜqūbī, II, 209; but cf. Ṭabarī, I, 3111 f.; *Fakhrī*, p. 119; Caetani, *op. cit.*, IX, 34.

sacred spot of Ḥijr, the ancient foundation of the temple of Mecca, supposedly laid by Abraham.[131] Ceremoniously she veiled. The people gathered around her. Her public address began:

O ye people! The rabble of the provinces, the men that wait at watering-places (to serve or rob), and the slaves of the people of Medina got together. The mob reproached him (ᶜUthmān), who was recently killed, for his cunning, for appointing young men to office while older ones had been appointed before him, and for protecting (for his party's use) some of the districts prohibited to them (the people). In these matters he had been preceded (by others), and it was not possible to do otherwise. He heeded them and desisted from these deeds, so as to conciliate them. But when they could find neither pretext nor excuse, they were agitated and began to show hostility. Their deeds were at variance with their words. They shed sacred blood, desecrated the sacred city, seized sacred funds, and profaned the sacred month. By Allah, ᶜUthmān's fingers are far better than a whole world full of the likes of them. Keep yourself safe by not associating with them, so that others can inflict an exemplary punishment on them and scatter in fright those who are behind them. By Allah, even if that which they imputed to him (ᶜUthmān) were indeed a fault, he has been purged of it as gold is purged of its dross or a garment of its dirt; for they rinsed him (in his own blood) as a garment is rinsed in water.

"Here I am," cried out Governor ᶜAbd Allah, "the first to demand revenge"; and so he became Aishah's first recruit for the civil war that was to follow.[132]

Aishah's choice of Mecca for her new headquarters was indeed the logical one. It was the slain caliph's "home town" and the ancient headquarters of the Quraish, which tribe now stood to lose a good deal of

[131] Yāqūt, *Geog.*, II, 208.

[132] Ṭabarī, I, 3096–98.

its power and prestige should the arrangements at Medina, engineered largely by non-Quraishites, be allowed to stand. Aishah's words, therefore, fell on fertile ground, and her followers grew rapidly in numbers. Prominent Umayyads of the city, others who had come from some of the provinces, and the fugitive group from Medina were only too ready to rally to the cause. Among the last group was Marwān ibn al-Ḥakam, who could not refrain from reminding the now weeping Aishah of the hostile role she had played in the events that finally led to ᶜUthmān's murder.[133] Even her own relative, ᶜUbaid, who was, however, a partisan of ᶜAlī, held her in part responsible for that murder.[134] In defense of herself and her seemingly contradictory words and deeds she explained that the rebels killed ᶜUthmān despite the fact that he had repented and that, though she had at first cried out against him, she had later (presumably on his repentance) changed her tone and attitude. Her last words, she claimed, were better than her first.[135] Time and again Aishah was to face such accusations, and their implication of insincerity and opportunism on her part, and always she was to insist on her innocence of the murder and her sincerity in the demand for its revenge.[136]

[133] Ṭabarī, I, 3075; ᶜ*Iqd*, II, 266.

[134] Ibn Saᶜd, V, 63 f.; Ṭabarī, I, 3111 f.

[135] Ṭabarī, I, 3112; *Fakhrī*, p. 119.

[136] E.g., Balādhurī, *Ansāb*, V, 101 f., 103; Ibn Saᶜd, III, 57; *Fakhrī*, p. 119; cf. below, pp. 165–72.

In the few months that followed ᶜAlī proved his own worst enemy. It soon became known that he *would* not—though he himself claimed that he *could* not—do anything to bring the regicides to justice. This lent more color to the accusation that he had had a hand in the murder of ᶜUthmān and so helped to undermine his popularity with some of the people. Still more detrimental to his cause was his determination to depose all of ᶜUthmān's provincial governors, including even Muᶜāwiyah, who had successfully ruled Syria for some twenty years. These he wished to replace by his own partisans. Men more experienced and farsighted than he pointed out to him the great danger of this move, but to no avail. "Remove all except Muᶜāwiyah," urged his counselors, only to be told, "I shall give Muᶜāwiyah nothing but the sword."[137] He thus threw into the arms of the opposition several of the dispossessed governors and roused the personal hostility of the shrewdest and ablest politician on the scene—Muᶜāwiyah. We have seen how ᶜAbd Allah, the governor of Mecca, was the first to respond to Aishah's call. A second ᶜAbd Allah ibn ᶜĀmir, ᶜUthmān's maternal cousin and his governor of Baṣrah, also headed for Mecca, where he joined forces with Aishah.[138] Yaᶜlā ibn Umayyah, ᶜUthmān's governor of the Yaman, was no sooner deposed than he got together all the revenue funds he could and departed for Mecca. There he too joined Aishah,

[137] Ṭabarī, I, 3082–86; cf. Caetani, *op. cit.*, IX, 13–15.

[138] Ṭabarī, I, 3057, 3099; Ibn Saᶜd, V, 31, 34.

placing his wealth and followers at the disposal of the opposition that she was so effectively bringing into existence.[139] As weeks yielded to months, ᶜAlī persisted in his policy of alienation; yet he took no steps to strengthen his position by any vigorous measures against the two-headed menace that was growing in Aishah's Ḥijāz and Muᶜāwiyah's Syria.

Muᶜāwiyah and his strong Umayyad party in Syria had early added their cries of revenge for ᶜUthmān's blood. But knowing his own strength in his province, Muᶜāwiyah, unlike the governors of Baṣrah and Yaman, stood guard in Syria. At first, most of ᶜAlī's demands that Muᶜāwiyah take the oath of allegiance went pointedly unanswered. It was most probably at this stage that Muᶜāwiyah was in secret correspondence with ᶜAlī's enemies, particularly with Zubair, inviting the latter to Syria and offering to recognize him as caliph.[140] Finally, some three months after ᶜUthmān's murder, they brought ᶜAlī a calculated insult, in the form of a blank letter, addressed simply "From Muᶜāwiyah to ᶜAlī." Muᶜāwiyah's man, however, was made to tell the Syrian story. "I left behind me," he said, "a people that will not be satisfied with anything short of revenge."

"Revenge on whom?" asked ᶜAlī.

"On you, yourself. Furthermore," he added, "I left behind me sixty thousand men weeping under the shirt of ᶜUthmān hung before them on the pulpit of

[139] Ṭabarī, I, 3089, 3099. [140] Cf. Caetani, *op. cit.*, IX, 157, 211.

(the Mosque of) Damascus."[141] For Muᶜāwiyah was quick to recognize the great propagandistic value of the blood-stained shirt of ᶜUthmān and the severed fingers of his wife Nāʾilah. These fingers were attached to the shirt, which was daily raised before the people to stir up their emotions and lead them to cry louder and louder for revenge on ᶜUthmān's murderers. Before these gruesome relics, many a man took oath to forego some pleasure or luxury—to approach no woman, to wash in no water (sand could be used), and to sleep on no bed—until the blood of ᶜUthmān was avenged. For one whole year, until the Battle of Ṣiffīn, these potent relics continued to render service.[142]

Muᶜāwiyah, however, was playing nobody's game but his own. In vain one searches for any evidence of genuine co-operation between him and Aishah's group. Both he and she, it is true, had the same cry of revenge on their lips, and both cherished personal animosity toward ᶜAlī. But beyond that, the son of Abū Sufyān and the daughter of Abū Bakr had little indeed in common. Mutual suspicions, even though suppressed, and conflicting ambitions, even though as yet unexpressed, prevented these two from taking the most likely step to insure ᶜAlī's defeat, namely, a well-timed march of Muᶜāwiyah's forces from the north and Aishah's forces from the south to meet and crush any military resistance on the part of ᶜAlī at Medina.

[141] Ṭabarī, I, 3090 f.

[142] *Ibid.*, p. 3255; cf. Caetani, *op. cit.*, IX, 233 f.

With the stakes of war as yet too indefinite, Muᶜāwiyah did not wish, for the sake of a joint victory, to risk an Egyptian invasion of Syria in his absence. And Aishah, who had at first hoped for much from Muᶜāwiyah and was at one time even prepared to join forces with him in Syria, was soon to be persuaded by her counselors that she need not expect any real co-operation from that source. Years later when Muᶜāwiyah had achieved the caliphate, he enumerated to ᶜAmr ibn al-ᶜĀṣ—the man who had done much to make that achievement possible—the four points that worked to his own advantage and to the disadvantage of ᶜAlī, making his victory over the latter possible. He specified as one of these four points his policy of letting ᶜAlī and Aishah with her group fight it out by themselves.[143]

Soon after the receipt of Muᶜāwiyah's blank letter, ᶜAlī began to think of invading Syria. Ṭalḥah and Zubair requested leave from him to go on a pilgrimage to Mecca. Though he had refused their previous requests to leave Medina, ᶜAlī, who had reason to suspect their loyalty, now let them go. So it happened that some four months after the unhappy murder of ᶜUthmān, Ṭalḥah, Zubair, and Aishah were once more together, with Aishah's residence their rendezvous. The two men could see for themselves the great party of insurrection already whipped into being by Aishah and her Meccan aids and advisers. To her inquiries as to the situation in Medina they were quick to an-

[143] ᶜ*Iqd*, II, 301.

swer, "We have fled from Medina, from the rabble, and from the Beduins. We parted from a perplexed people that neither acknowledge the right nor disavow the false; nor do they restrain themselves."

"Consult over this affair and rise against this rabble," said Aishah, reinforcing her advice by quoting:

> Were the leaders of my people in accord with me
> I would deliver them from the rope-halters and from ruin.[144]

The leaders were divided on the course to be followed. Some wished to proceed directly against ᶜAlī in Medina, while others advised going to Syria. Aishah was seemingly willing to follow either course. But the weight of opinion inclined in favor of the latter until the former governor of Baṣrah, ᶜAbd Allah ibn ᶜĀmir, advised against it and proposed instead that they go to Baṣrah. His argument was that Muᶜāwiyah was sufficient for the cause in Syria[145] or that Muᶜāwiyah would not be led by them or indeed co-operate with them.[146] On the other hand, he pointed out, he himself had friends and influence in Baṣrah, where Ṭalḥah too had a following. Aishah was won over to the new plan and was urged to go with them to stir up the people of Baṣrah for the cause as she had so successfully roused the people of Mecca.[147]

The decision once arrived at, it was soon an-

[144] Ṭabarī, I, 3099, 3102. [145] *Ibid.*, p. 3099.

[146] Masᶜūdī, *Murūj al-Dhahab* (*Les Prairies d'Or*), ed. C. Barbier de Meynard (9 vols.; Paris, 1861–77).

[147] Ṭabarī, I, 3099 f.

nounced by a public crier who informed the Meccans that the Mother of the Believers was departing to Baṣrah to avenge the blood of ʿUthmān. Those who wished to join her but had neither mount nor funds were promised these necessities. About a thousand in all, including many of the Quraish, answered that call. Those of Aishah's "sisters" that were in Mecca at that time had intended to return with her to Medina. But when it was decided to go to Baṣrah, they, except for Ḥafṣah, did not wish to follow her. They accompanied the party to near-by Dhāt ʿIrq,[148] and there, with such weeping as was never heard before or after for and in Islam, they bid Aishah goodbye. That ominous day came to be known as the "Day of Weeping."[149]

Aishah's leadership had placed the rest of the Mothers of the Believers in an uneasy position. Some of them seem to have given silent consent to her plans. The Umayyad Umm Ḥabībah most probably shared her half-brother Muʿāwiyah's views of the whole movement. Only Ḥafṣah, Aishah's old partner in harem intrigues, wished to go the whole way with her friend. She was, however, prevented from accompanying Aishah to Baṣrah by her brother, ʿAbd Allah, who wished to return to Medina so as to be guided by the decisions and actions of the leaders of that city.[150] On the other hand, Umm Salamah, who even in Mohammed's time had championed the cause of Fāṭi-

[148] Yāqūt, III, 652, 574.

[149] Ṭabarī, I, 3100, 3114.

[150] *Ibid.*, pp. 3101, 3105, 3113.

mah and ᶜAlī and had identified herself with the People of the (prophet's) House, took a definite stand against Aishah. She continued her return journey to Medina at the time that Aishah, and presumably the rest of Mohammed's widows, cut their journey short to return once again to Mecca.[151]

Yaᶜqūbī's account, generally favorable to the ᶜAlīds, represents Aishah as taking the initiative in approaching Umm Salamah and soliciting her cooperation. He places the incident in Mecca *after* the arrival of Ṭalḥah and Zubair in that city.[152] If Aishah and Umm Salamah indeed had such an interview, it most probably took place in the initial stages of Aishah's revolt, perhaps just *before* the two parted company at Sarif. For Aishah must have instinctively known the futility of any such appeal (to her former rival and known friend of ᶜAlī) at so late a stage in the development of her plans, when military revolt against ᶜAlī was deemed necessary. Besides, there is no confirmation of Umm Salamah's presence at Mecca at this stage, while the following incidents point to her presence in Medina. ᶜAlī was immediately informed of Aishah's new plan by a special messenger sent from Mecca by Umm al-Faḍl, who was both his sister-in-law and the wife of ᶜAbbās.[153] Sizing up the increased menace of an open revolt led by Aishah and her group of outstanding men whose influence ᶜAlī

[151] Balādhurī, *Ansāb*, V, 91 f.

[152] Yaᶜqūbī, II, 209 f.

[153] ᶜ*Iqd*, II, 281; *Aghānī*, XI, 125; Ibn Ḥanbal, VI, 228.

was well aware of,[154] he gave up the idea of marching north against Muᶜāwiyah, and decided instead to intercept Aishah's party on its way to Baṣrah.[155] Umm Salamah came to him to offer the services of her son. "O Commander of the Believers," she said, "were it not disobeying Allah Almighty and you would not accept it from me, I would go with you. But here is my son, ᶜUmar—Allah knows he is more precious to me than my soul—to go with you."[156] Having decided to stay home as befits a God-fearing gentlewoman, Umm Salamah next wrote Aishah, urging her to desist from the unrighteous and unwomanly course that she, a Mother of the Believers, was then following. This widow of Mohammed expressed her pious and firm conviction that Aishah's conduct would not meet with Mohammed's approval and that woman's place was at home and not on the battlefield. But it is too much to expect that Aishah, having already gone so far, would be influenced by anything Umm Salamah had to say. Her curt reply was pointedly headed, "From Aishah, the Mother of the Believers, to Umm Salamah." A literal translation of the letter fails to convey all the irony and defiance implied in the classic note, of which Professor Sprengling gives the following free translation:

What an honor indeed to receive your sermon! How well I know your right to advise me! I am not making the Lesser Pilgrimage (ᶜ*Umrah*) as a casual visitor. An excellent vantage

[154] See above, p. 128.

[155] Ṭabarī, I, 3101, 3106.

[156] *Ibid.*, p. 3101.

point is a vantage point in which I distinguish between two parties of Moslems at variance with one another. If I stay put, it will not be because of any constraint. If I go away, then it will be for something about which I need not expatiate any further. Goodbye.[157]

ᶜAskar, the camel that carried Aishah on her momentous expedition, was one of the best that Arabia could provide. It was bought from an owner who valued it above any mare, but who readily offered it as a free gift, once he knew it was being sought for the Mother of the Believers. The offer, however, was no more than a graceful gesture, for Yaᶜlā, rich and foremost in his contribution to the cause, paid a handsome price for the animal.[158]

Before Aishah's avenging army of some three thousand had left Mecca behind them, there occurred the first of a series of events on that journey that reflected the personal rivalries and ambitions of those in her camp. Marwān raised the question of leadership in prayer. ᶜAbd Allah felt that his father, Zubair, should lead; but Ṭalḥah's son, Mohammed, thought his father should be given that honor. Aishah, sensing conflict and suspecting Marwān's motive, rebuked the latter and forestalled any trouble by a quick decision. "Do you wish," she said to Marwān, "to divide us? Let my sister's son (ᶜAbd Allah) lead in prayer," which he did until they reached Baṣrah.[159]

157 ᶜ*Iqd*, II, 277.

158 Ṭabarī, I, 3102 f., 3108 f.; cf. Caetani, *op. cit.*, IX, 54 f.

159 Ṭabarī, I, 3105 f.

As already stated, Aishah's "sisters" parted company from her at Dhāt ᶜIrq. An even more significant group deserted Aishah's cause either at that point or at Marr al-Ẓahrān, some five miles from Mecca.[160] Here several private conferences took place between some of the leading men. Saᶜīd ibn al-ᶜĀṣ, ᶜUthmān's former governor of Kūfah,[161] was for striking down ᶜUthmān's murderers—and he implied these were none other than their companions Ṭalḥah and Zubair—then and there with the sword and so be done with the avenging of the blood of ᶜUthmān. But Marwān counseled otherwise. His plan was the age-old one of divide and conquer, for he wished to stir one party against the other so as to profit by the death of the fallen and the weakness, if not the exhaustion, of the victors, who could then be easily overcome.[162] Saᶜīd now wanted to make sure who and what he was to fight for. He approached Ṭalḥah and Zubair, wishing to know who, in the event of victory, would be their candidate. They answered, "One of us two, whichever one the people should prefer." He argued that, since they claimed they wished only to avenge ᶜUthmān, it would be more appropriate to have one of ᶜUthmān's sons as a candidate. They, in their turn, pointed out the inappropriateness of passing over the older men, Mohammed's immigrant companions, in favor of

[160] Yāqūt, IV, 494.

[161] See above, pp. 112 f.

[162] Ṭabarī, I, 3103; Ibn Saᶜd, V, 23 f.; cf. also Ṭabarī, II, 164; Wellhausen, *The Arab Kingdom and Its Fall*, p. 136, for another instance of Marwān's use of this method.

these men's sons. Said Saᶜīd, "I do not see myself fighting to divert it (the caliphate) from the sons of ᶜAbd Manāf (Umayyads)." With that, he decided to leave the camp. Soon others, including Mughīrah ibn Shuᶜbah, followed suit and with them went also their followers.[163]

The defection of such groups from her cause, her suspicions of Marwān, and her awareness of the undercurrent of rivalry between Ṭalḥah and Zubair must have had a depressing effect on Aishah, perhaps even conditioning her reaction to the next reported incident of the journey. Passing by the watering spring of Ḥauʾāb, Aishah heard either barking or more probably howling of dogs. For barking dogs are common enough and excite but little attention; howling dogs, on the other hand, are considered by the superstitious Arabs as an ill omen. It may have been, therefore, no more than a case of superstitious fear following after the disturbing and thought-provoking events already recorded that caused Aishah to hesitate in her course and to wish to return to Mecca. Be that as it may, traditions generally unfavorable to Aishah give a different explanation of her agitated reaction. They state that she recalled in a flash a prediction of Mohammed's about the dogs of Ḥauʾāb. Most of these traditions make Aishah report Mohammed's words, addressed to his wives, as follows: "O that I knew which one of you it is at whom the dogs

[163] Ṭabarī, I, 3103 f.; Ibn Saᶜd, V, 23 f.; cf. Nawawī, p. 281; cf. below, p. 168.

of Ḥauʾāb will bark!"[164] One version has Mohammed, addressing himself to Aishah alone, say, "Let it not be you at whom the dogs of Ḥauʾāb will bark."[165] Still another version, obviously Shīʿite, makes him say to her, "O Fair one, it is as if I see it to be you at whom the dogs of Ḥauʾāb bark, and you fighting ʿAlī unjustly!"[166] Aishah had dismounted and refused to continue with the journey. Zubair and others, anxious to move on, swore to her that the guide had mistaken the place and that they were not at Ḥauʾāb at all. But Aishah heeded them not. A whole day passed. Desperate, they gave the false alarm that ʿAlī was close upon them. Only then did they get this Mother of the Believers, now so essential to their undertaking, to quiet her own inner doubts and fears and to resume her march.[167]

Arrived at the outskirts of Baṣrah, Ibn ʿĀmir was sent ahead to prepare the way, since he, as former governor of that city, knew its people and its ways. Aishah also at this time wrote letters to several of the leading men in Baṣrah, calling them to the cause. ʿUthmān ibn Ḥunaif, ʿAlī's new governor of Baṣrah, sent two messengers to ascertain the insurgents' objective. They were received first by Aishah, who

[164] Ṭabarī, I, 3127; Ibn al-Athīr, III, 169 f.; Abū al-Fidā, I, 290; Ibn Ḥanbal, VI, 97; Yāqūt, II, 353; cf. Muir, *op. cit.*, p. 242; Caetani, *op. cit.*, IX, 54–56 and 84, where he suggests the incident is a later invention.

[165] Yaʿqūbī, II, 210.

[166] ʿ*Iqd*, II, 283 f.; cf. Caetani, *op. cit.*, IX, 210, sec. 277.

[167] Ṭabarī, I, 3109, and n. 164 above.

showed herself ready to inform "her sons." She enumerated the evil happenings at Medina. These, she said, she wished to make known to the rest of the uninformed Moslems. Their objectives, she claimed, were the avenging of the blood of ᶜUthmān and setting things right in Islam. Ever ready with citation from the poets and the Qur'ān, she now called into good use a verse from the latter: "There is no good in much confidential talk with them except those who urge alms-giving or reputable conduct or setting things right among the people."[168] The messengers next interviewed Ṭalḥah and Zubair, who stated they were at one with Aishah in their aims and cleared themselves of any disloyalty to ᶜAlī by insisting that they had taken the oath of allegiance to him under compulsion. Before returning to the governor of Baṣrah, the two messengers came back to take their leave of Aishah, who sent them on their way with a second Qur'ānic citation for a parting word: "Be ye furnishers of justice, witnesses of Allah, even though it be against yourselves or your parents and relatives. . . . . So do not follow desire so as to waver."[169]

ᶜUthmān, after an interview with his returned messengers, called on the people of Baṣrah to resist the invaders. He soon discovered that these latter had some strong support in his city, thanks no doubt to the influence and efforts of his predecessor in office, Ibn ᶜĀmir. Nevertheless, he and his supporters went

[168] Sūrah 4:114.

[169] Sūrah 4:134; Ṭabarī, I, 3115–17; Ibn al-Athīr, III, 170 f.

out to meet and fight the rebels, who had in the meantime taken their position at the Mirbad quarter, or market, of the city.[170] First Ṭalḥah and then Zubair made their speeches, which were favorably received by some but resented by others. Presently the Baṣrans were throwing pebbles or stones at one another, and a small riot was in the making. It was then that Aishah came to the rescue with her speech. Though not a large woman, she yet had a powerful voice, that generally commanded attention. She recounted how in the past people had come to her at Medina with their complaints against ʿUthmān; how they soon overstepped the bounds of truth and justice, acting from other than their avowed motives; how in their excesses they attacked ʿUthmān in his house; how they shed (his) sacred blood, seized sacred funds, and violated the sacred city, all without any cause or excuse. There was nothing for them left to do, she urged, but to bring the regicides to justice and to be guided by the Book of Allah Almighty. "Have you not seen," she cited the Qurʾān in conclusion, "those to whom a portion of the Book has been given being called to the Book of Allah that it might judge between them?"[171]

This short but effective speech divided the followers of ʿUthmān ibn Ḥunaif into two factions. There were those who said Aishah had indeed spoken the truth and meant well. But there were also those who, giving the first faction the lie, censured her for

[170] Yāqūt, IV, 484. [171] Sūrah 3:22.

assuming public leadership and thus violating the seclusion imposed upon Mohammed's wives.[172] Night forestalled major action.

The whole of the next day saw severe fighting between ᶜAlī's loyalists and ᶜUthmān's avengers, with the former losing so heavily that they sued for truce. The terms agreed on were that ᶜUthmān was to retain possession of Baṣrah and that a messenger was to be sent to Medina to ascertain if Ṭalḥah and Zubair had indeed taken the oath of allegiance to ᶜAlī under compulsion. If the people of Medina confirmed the claim of compulsion, then ᶜUthmān was to deliver Baṣrah to Ṭalḥah and Zubair, but if the Medinans denied any compulsion, then Aishah and her party were to depart from Baṣrah. Kaᶜb ibn Sūr (or Shūr), of whom more presently, was found acceptable to both parties as the man for this mission. He found at Medina a difference of opinion on this now all-important question.[173]

In the meantime, ᶜAlī with some three thousand men had left the City of the Prophet (late in October, 656) in the hope of overtaking the insurgents at Rabadhah, some few miles northeast of Medina.[174] He had not moved fast enough to accomplish that purpose and so continued on the way to ᶜIrāq, with Kūfah as his destination. News of the Baṣran truce and its terms reached him on the way. He therefore

[172] Ṭabarī, I, 3118–20; Ibn al-Athīr, III, 172.

[173] Ṭabarī, I, 3123–26; Ibn al-Athīr, III, 173–75.

[174] Yāqūt, II, 448 f.; Ṭabarī, I, 3106.

sent ᶜUthmān a letter denying that any compulsion was used on either Ṭalḥah or Zubair. ᶜUthmān decided to stand by ᶜAlī and called on the rebels to depart. The latter in their turn claimed that Kaᶜb's report justified them in their demand that ᶜUthmān himself evacuate the city. That evening under cover of darkness and pretext of evening prayer the rebels entered the mosque, staged a surprise attack on ᶜUthmān and his party, routed them, and took ᶜUthmān himself prisoner. Some wished to put him to death, but Aishah intervened to set him free. The unhappy man was flogged in public and was put to the further indignity of having his head and beard shaved and his eyebrows and lashes plucked. It was in this tragicomic condition that he found his way to his master ᶜAlī, who was still on his way to ᶜIrāq.[175]

The victorious rebels were not disposed to be lenient with their defeated enemies. They put some of the leaders to death and flogged others to intimidate the rest, of whom many were forced into hiding.[176] In the opinion of some the blood of ᶜUthmān had been sufficiently avenged. That opinion, however, was not shared by the victors.

The conquest of Baṣrah, as its former governor, Ibn ᶜĀmir, had expected, thus proved a comparatively easy undertaking. But there was yet much to be accomplished before the victors could attain their real and primarily personal ambitions. Hitherto these had been masked, for the most part, behind the general

[175] Ṭabarī, I, 3126, 3143 f.

[176] *Ibid.*, pp. 3127–30.

cry of revenge for ᶜUthmān's blood. That cry still persisted, but it was now becoming more boldly associated with the demand for the deposition of ᶜAlī,[177] which would, in its turn, open the way for the election of either Ṭalḥah or Zubair as caliph. But, before challenging the enemy again, the victors had to come to some understanding among themselves. Their Baṣran partisans took the oath to both Ṭalḥah and Zubair, who were in joint command.[178] Aishah's brother, ᶜAbd al-Raḥmān, was placed over the public treasury.[179] The ticklish question of leadership in prayer was once more raised. Aishah, according to one version, again decided in favor of her nephew ᶜAbd Allah, the son of Zubair; but a second account states that she had ᶜAbd Allah and Mohammed, the son of Ṭalḥah, lead in prayers on alternate days.[180]

The tasks before them now were to consolidate their position in Baṣrah itself, to win near-by Kūfah to their cause, and to secure recognition and, if need be, aid from the provinces. Both parties had to reckon with leading individuals, subtribes, or entire tribes in ᶜIrāq that wished to be neutral under the perplexing circumstances that would force them to fight either Mohammed's widow and closest friends, on the one hand, or the cousin and son-in-law of the prophet, on the other. The case of Kaᶜb ibn Sūr gives some idea of how Aishah applied herself to this problem.

[177] *Ibid.*, pp. 3135 f., 3125; Ibn al-Athīr, III, 176; cf. above, pp. 142 f.

[178] Ṭabarī, I, 3136.

[179] *Ibid.*, p. 3135.

[180] *Ibid.*; Yaᶜqūbī, II, 210 f.; Ibn Saᶜd, V, 39; cf. above, p. 141.

Kaᶜb was a judge of Baṣrah and a member of the tribe of Azd. He had been sent, as was stated above, to Medina to ascertain the conditions under which Ṭalḥah and Zubair had taken the oath of allegiance to ᶜAlī. The realization that Medina was divided on the question may have influenced him to take a neutral position on his return to Baṣrah, where he now is found advising his own tribe and its chief, Ṣabrah ibn Shaimān, to do the same.[181] He himself retired into the seclusion of his own house. Aishah was made to realize that he was the key man of the Azd and must be won over if that tribe was to be on her side. Since he would not leave his house, Aishah herself went to call on him. He refused to speak to her at first. "O Kaᶜb," she cried, "am I not your Mother, and have claims on you?" Her "son" listened. She persuaded him she merely wanted to set things right and soon won his support.[182] But not even she could win all the Baṣrans over to her side. As the days passed and the showdown drew near, the Baṣrans fell into three groups: those that were with her and her party, those that were with ᶜAlī, and those that insisted on remaining neutral.[183] Outstanding among the last group was Aḥnaf ibn Qais, of the tribe of Tamīm, who with a large number of tribesmen left Baṣrah to retire to a near-by valley.[184]

[181] Ṭabarī, I, 3178.

[182] Ibn Saᶜd, VII¹, 65 f.; Dīnawarī, p. 153.

[183] Ṭabarī, I, 3178 f.

[184] *Ibid.*, pp. 3168–71, 3174, 3178 f.; Ibn al-Athīr, III, 195 f.; ᶜ*Iqd*, II, 278 f.

The effort to win the Kūfans over to her side or at least to persuade them against actively joining ᶜAlī had to be carried out, at first, by correspondence. Here Aishah was again approaching leading individuals as well as the Kūfans in general. Her letters sought to justify her position, revealed a frustrated plot on her life, described the victory at Baṣrah, and called on the Kūfans for their support.[185] These efforts coincided with similar ones on the part of ᶜAlī, who sent three successive pairs of envoys to Kūfah to propagandize that city and to line up its governor, Abū Mūsā, on his side.[186] Those selected for this important mission were, first, Aishah's brother Mohammed and ᶜAlī's own nephew, Mohammed ibn Jaᶜfar. The two Mohammeds approached Abū Mūsā and found him more interested in the orderly punishment of the regicides than in rushing to arms on the side of either ᶜAlī or Aishah. They returned to report their failure to ᶜAlī, who then sent his general Ashtar and his cousin Ibn al-ᶜAbbās to reason with Abū Mūsā, who owed his high office largely to Ashtar's efforts.[187] But the latter was determined to remain neutral and made every effort in public speeches and subsequent debates on the order of a "town

[185] Ṭabarī, I, 3115, 3132–34; Ibn al-Athīr, III, 178.

[186] Cf. Caetani, *op. cit.*, IX, 220, where the author questions the role assigned to the different ones involved in these events at Mecca. There may be room to question some of the details, but there can be no doubt that there was a strong neutral party in Kūfah and that ᶜAlī and his best men had to work hard and fast to overcome it.

[187] Yaᶜqūbī, II, 208; cf. above, p. 113.

meeting" to convince the Kūfans that this was an evil civil war and they would do well by themselves and their faith to leave it strictly alone. Again ᶜAlī's messengers reported the failure of their mission. The caliph made one more effort to counteract Abū Mūsā's influence and gain the support of the Kūfans. He sent them this time his own son Ḥasan and his right-hand man and former governor of Kūfah, ᶜAmmār ibn Yāsir. The latter was particularly anxious to prevent any of the Kūfans from going over to Aishah, whose influence, he was aware, was great. He, therefore, though acknowledging her high station in this world and the next as the wife of Mohammed, nevertheless warned his hearers that Allah was using her to put them through a severe test to see if they would obey her or him.[188] He and his companion, however, made no headway with the Kūfan governor, who, to justify his neutral attitude, cited freely the word of Allah forbidding strife and bloodshed among the believers:

> O ye who have believed, do not consume your property among you in vanity and do not kill each other. . . . . If anyone kill a believer intentionally, his recompense is Gehenna, to abide therein; Allah will be angry with him and will curse him and prepare for him a mighty punishment.[189]

ᶜAmmār was bold in his counterspeeches. He derided Abū Mūsā and called on himself rough talk from the

[188] Bukhārī, IV, 376 f.; ᶜ*Iqd*, II, 276, 283; Ṭabarī, I, 3150.

[189] Sūrah 2:33 and 95; Ṭabarī, I, 3139–47, 3155; Ibn al-Athīr, III, 181–85; ᶜ*Iqd*, II, 276.

governor's supporters. Abū Mūsā threaded his way through the angry crowd to the mosque and mounted the pulpit still bent on making pacific and neutral speeches.

In the meantime, Zaid ibn Ṣūḥān, of the tribe of ᶜAbd al-Qais, who had been among the Kūfan opponents of ᶜUthmān,[190] and one of the leaders approached by Aishah, took a hand in the affair. Aishah's letter to him had read: "From Aishah, the daughter of Abū Bakr, Mother of the Believers, Beloved of the Messenger of Allah—to her faithful son Zaid ibn Ṣūḥān. To proceed. When this my letter reaches you, come and help us in our undertaking. If you do not do that, then turn the people away from following ᶜAlī." His answer had been: "I am your faithful son provided you refrain from this undertaking and return to your home; otherwise I shall be the first to thwart you."[191] Her general letter to the Kūfans had called on them to remain in their homes and refrain from action except against the murderers of ᶜUthmān. Taking both letters with him, Zaid, seated on his mount, took his position at the entrance of the mosque and, having read the last letter, made his little speech. "She (Aishah) was given a command and we too were given a command. She was ordered to stay in her home and we were ordered to fight to prevent sedition. Now she commands us to do what she herself was ordered to do while she rides

[190] Ṭabarī, I, 2921, 2954, 3034.

[191] *Ibid.*, p. 3137; Ibn al-Athīr, III, 174 f.; ᶜ*Iqd*, II, 277.

to carry out the orders given to us." This brought Shabath ibn Ribʿī to Aishah's defense: "You stole and Allah cut off your hand. You disobey the Mother of the Believers and Allah will strike you dead.[192] She has not commanded except that which Allah most high has commanded, namely, the setting of things right among the people." Abū Mūsā was still striving to lead the Kūfans into the path of neutrality, while Zaid proclaimed that such a path was now no more possible than the turning of the waters of the Euphrates back to its source.[193]

But while these speeches and counterspeeches were going on in the mosque, Ashtar had once more arrived on the scene at Kūfah. He bid all he met on his way to follow him to the governor's palace of which he took quick and bold possession. Two of Abū Mūsā's palace boys presently brought news of Ashtar's exploit. To Abū Mūsā this meant the loss of his fight for neutrality. A large Kūfan army, led by Zaid and Ashtar among others, started on its way by land and by the Euphrates to join ʿAlī's forces encamped at Dhū Qār.[194]

Despite this powerful addition to his forces, ʿAlī, who for more than one reason was anxious to avoid open warfare, set a peace movement afoot by dispatching one of the Kūfan leaders, Qaʿqāʿ ibn ʿAmr,

[192] Zaid was among those who fell fighting against Aishah (cf. Ṭabarī, I, 3147–49, 3192).

[193] *Ibid.*, pp. 3147–49; cf. Caetani, *op. cit.*, IX, 97.

[194] Ṭabarī, I, 3152–55, 3172 f.

to talk matters over with the insurgents at Baṣrah. According to some accounts, ʿAlī had previously sent Ibn al- Abbās to Baṣrah with instructions to see Zubair alone and to call him back to his allegiance. It seems that ʿAlī considered Zubair the more reasonable of his two rivals and blamed Zubair's son, ʿAbd Allah, for the father's desertion to Aishah's group. There was, however, nothing pacific about Zubair's answer to that move.[195] Qaʿqāʿ was seemingly to have better luck. Arrived at Baṣrah, he, like ʿUthmān ibn Ḥunaif's envoys, made his way straight to Aishah, who assured him, as she had done Kaʿb ibn Sūr, that she wished only to set things right among the people. He then asked her to send for Ṭalḥah and Zubair so she could hear what he and they had to say. The two were called, and Qaʿqāʿ won an admission from them that they were one with Aishah in their desires. Asked for a more specific statement of their aims, they are said to have mentioned only the punishment of the regicides. Now ʿAlī had at no time denied the guilt of the regicides, though he had pointed out that their effective punishment was not within his ready reach. His envoy, therefore, pointed out to his listeners that if they would but declare allegiance to ʿAlī, due punishment of the regicides would follow upon the restoration of the resulting peace, order, and unity. He added further that they had already shed much blood to avenge that of ʿUthmān, and that in so doing they had roused many others to cry for revenge

[195] ʿ*Iqd*, II, 276.

for the blood of their recently slain kinsmen. In short, he strove to convince them that they were about to embark on something that was far bigger in scope and more evil in character than they had anticipated. The record goes on to say that they then asked Qaᶜqāᶜ to return and ascertain if ᶜAlī was indeed of the same mind as he, in which event the matter could be settled peaceably.[196]

It must not be supposed that it was the logic of Qaᶜqāᶜ's argument alone that induced his listeners to consider a possible conciliation. There was also the knowledge of their own comparative weakness in ᶜIrāq now that the Kūfan majority had declared for ᶜAlī, while Baṣrah itself was torn three ways. Furthermore, Aishah's letters, sent after the conquest of Baṣrah to Syria, Medina, and Yamāmah in the Najd, had brought no military aid and little, if any, moral support.[197] The key province of the Ḥijāz remained quiet, as did also the Umayyad stronghold, Syria, where Muᶜāwiyah was playing the game of watchful waiting. It is a question, too, as to how much genuine co-operation and unity of purpose there was right there in Aishah's camp between her and her rival family candidates, on the one hand, and Marwān and his Umayyads, on the other. It is to be noted in this connection that none of the Umayyad leaders were present at the interview with Qaᶜqāᶜ nor were they consulted on the new policy of possible reconciliation.

[196] Ṭabarī, I, 3156–58; Ibn al-Athīr, III, 189–91.

[197] Ṭabarī, I, 3131 f., 3152; Ibn al-Athīr, III, 178, 187.

Qaᶜqāᶜ reported back to ᶜAlī, who advanced on Baṣrah and resumed the peace negotiations in person. The two armies came in sight of each other on the outskirts of the city at a place called Khuraibah. Aishah is credited with making quite a speech to the Baṣrans.[198] This probably took place sometime in the three-day interval between the sighting of the enemy and the day of actual battle. The rival forces kept to camp for these three days while negotiations were in progress. ᶜAlī rode out to talk matters over with Ṭalḥah and Zubair. Rumor spread in both camps that a reconciliation was in sight. How well founded this rumor was is difficult to tell, and it is not easy to discover the probable terms of the anticipated reconciliation, for the accounts that have come down to us of the interviews between ᶜAlī and his chief opponents have been colored by later sentiments. These portray Ṭalḥah and Zubair as conscience-stricken and repentant. ᶜAlī is made to find fault more with Zubair's son ᶜAbd Allah (the future challenger of the Umayyads) than with Zubair himself.[199] Aishah, quite unlike herself, has nothing to say when Zubair informs her of his desire to quit and go his way. The relationship between ᶜAbd Allah and his father—still according to these traditions—was on the verge of an open break when the former, alarmed at his father's sudden desire for peace, hurled at him a vehement accusation of

[198] ᶜ*Iqd*, II, 190, 276 f.

[199] Cf., e.g., Dīnawarī, p. 156, where it is stated that the Baṣrans did not respond to ᶜAlī's peace moves.

cowardice.[200] There is some evidence, however, of active rivalry between Ṭalḥah and Zubair even at this stage, and also some that Zubair wished to join Muʿāwiyah, who had previously promised to support his candidacy.[201]

There was in ʿAlī's camp a group that had good reason to fear a genuine peace movement. These were the regicides and others who were involved, directly or indirectly, in the murder of ʿUthmān. Among their leaders was ʿAlī's general, Ashtar. Most of the sources pass over in silence the immediate cause of the outbreak of hostilities between the two armies whose chiefs were reported on the verge of a happy reconciliation. Some, however, place the entire responsibility for the outbreak on this comparatively small group of regicides who are said to have made a surprise attack on the unsuspecting Baṣran camp.[202]

The two opposing armies crossed swords early in the morning on Thursday, the fourth of December, 656 (10 Jamadā II, 36).[203] Kaʿb ibn Sūr led Aishah to the scene of attack in the hope that her presence and influence might yet avert a major clash.[204] Seated in a mail-covered red pavilion mounted on her own camel, ʿAskar, Aishah went into the midst of the fray. But it

[200] Ṭabarī, I, 3175 f., 3181; Ibn al-Athīr, III, 196–98; cf. Caetani, *op. cit.*, IX, 222.

[201] Cf. Caetani, *op. cit.*, IX, 157, and above, p. 134.

[202] Ṭabarī, I, 3162–65, 3182 f.; Caetani, *op. cit.*, IX, 178 f., 222.

[203] Ṭabarī, I, 3218; cf. Caetani, *op. cit.*, IX, 166 f.

[204] Ṭabarī, I, 3183; Ibn al-Athīr, III, 199; Ibn ʿAsākir, VII, 84.

was of no use. The fight was on in earnest, and the Baṣrans were getting so much the worst of it that they began to take to flight. It was then that Aishah, herself no coward, rose to the emergency of the situation. She ordered Kaᶜb to leave her and approach the front ranks with cries for peace and the judgment of the Qurʾān, giving him, according to some versions, her own copy of the sacred text[205] to raise aloft and secure the attention and hoped-for compliance of the fighters. But Kaᶜb was immediately shot down by an arrow. Aishah herself strove valiantly to halt the flight and rally her forces with loud and repeated cries of, "O my sons, endurance! Remember Allah Most High and the Reckoning." When this failed to stop the flight, she tried once again, this time with a curse on the murderers of ᶜUthmān and their followers. The fighters picked up the curse for a battle cry as it were and returned to the attack. Like a general ordering his forces, she sent word to her commanders to hold fast their positions.[206] Her party's forces were in desperate need of an able commander-in-general. From the start neither Ṭalḥah nor Zubair had proved equal to the situation. The accounts (no doubt somewhat colored) of their conduct on this occasion are not very flattering to either their military ability or their personal courage.

It is not surprising, then, that the severest fighting now centered round Aishah and her camel. Fearless

[205] Ṭabarī, I, 3211; Ibn ᶜAsākir, VII, 85.

[206] Ṭabarī, I, 3191, 3211 f; Ibn al-Athīr, III, 201; Ibn ᶜAsākir, VII, 84 f.

herself, this Mother of the Believers roundly denounced strife and cowardice, on the one hand,[207] while, on the other, she continued to incite her warriors to heroic action with battle cries and martial poetry much after the fashion of the pagan "lady of victory" of pre-Islamic days, whose capture in battle meant certain defeat.[208] Thick and fast flew the arrows around her red pavilion. Several groups of her warriors outdid others in their courageous defense of her. Among these were the Banū Ḍabbah and their cousins, the Banū ᶜAdī, to which belonged the family of ᶜUmar ibn al-Khaṭṭāb.[209] One after another of her valiant believing "sons" rushed to take hold of the bridle of her camel, to defend her at the risk of their own lives, and to challenge and fight the enemy with frenzied valor. Many were the sons (seventy is the usual number given) who thus won a hero's death at this Battle of the Camel, as it came to be called.[210] This slaughter around her camel soon came to be proverbial.[211] Among those who fell was Mohammed, the son of Ṭalḥah.[212] ᶜAbd Allah, the son of Zubair, engaged ᶜAlī's general, Ashtar, in personal combat.[213]

[207] Cf. ᶜ*Iqd*, I, 37, 52.

[208] Cf. Abbott, "Women and the State on the Eve of Islam," *AJSL*, LVIII (1941), 262 f., 274, 280.

[209] Ṭabarī, I, 3177, 3196–98, 3224; ᶜ*Iqd*, II, 281, 47; Masᶜūdī, IV, 326.

[210] Ṭabarī, I, 3186; Ibn Saᶜd, IV², 27.

[211] Cf. Ibn Saᶜd, VII¹, 118 f.

[212] Ṭabarī, I, 3208, 3228; Ibn Saᶜd, V, 39.

[213] Ibn Taghrībirdī, I, 117–19; Ṭabarī, I, 3200, 3207; Ibn Khallikān, *Biographical Dictionary*, trans. W. M. de Slane (4 vols.; Paris, 1843–71), IV, 536.

Though he escaped with his life, he on that day received no less than some forty wounds.[214] ᶜAlī, realizing the role of Aishah on her camel, gave orders to hamstring the animal.[215] The disabled creature fell and with it fell all of Aishah's hopes. Her personal courage had availed little. The battle was lost and with it was lost also her cause. Her party was now once again in flight, and presently her two candidates themselves were to perish.

Ṭalḥah, about to leave the scene of defeat, was shot down by an arrow said to have been deliberately aimed at him by Marwān, who, holding him partly responsible for the murder of ᶜUthmān, thought thus to avenge the slain caliph.[216] That Marwān was capable of such a deed is not improbable. That he actually did it, however, is disputed not so much by the Moslem sources themselves[217] as by modern scholars, who with some justification suspect later anti-Umayyad propaganda as the source of the assertion.[218] Zubair, wounded, retired from the fight. Passing by the encampment of Aḥnaf ibn Qais, he was recognized, followed, and treacherously murdered.[219]

[214] Ṭabarī, I, 3199 f.; Ibn ᶜAsākir, VII, 402.

[215] Ṭabarī, I, 3200; but see *ibid.*, pp. 3204, 3209; Dīnawarī, p. 160; cf. Della Vida, "Il Califato ....," *op. cit.*, pp. 444 f.

[216] Ṭabarī, I, 3186; Ibn al-Athīr, III, 200; Ibn Saᶜd, III, 158 f.; *ibid*, V, 26; ᶜ*Iqd*, II, 279; *Ansāb*, V, 126; Yaᶜqūbī, II, 212; Masᶜūdī, IV, 321; Dīnawarī, p. 159; etc.

[217] E.g., Ibn ᶜAsākir (VII, 85) goes as far as to say that Marwān confessed shooting the arrow.

[218] E.g., Caetani, *op. cit.*, IX, 81, 224.

[219] Ṭabarī, I, 3187 f.; Ibn al-Athīr, III, 200 f.; Dīnawarī, pp. 157 f.

Though Aishah's red pavilion was at the end of the battle so thickly pierced with arrows that it was compared to a hedgehog,[220] she herself escaped with no more than a slight scratch or two inflicted by some of these arrows.[221] Soon after her camel fell, her brother Mohammed and ᶜAmmār, among a few others, rushed to her side. They cut her pavilion loose and carried her in it away from the crowd. ᶜAmmār, though protecting the "beloved of Mohammed" from the insults of the vulgar,[222] did, nevertheless, take this opportunity to rebuke his "Mother" for shedding the blood of her "sons"; and she in her turn disowned him as her "son."[223] Presently ᶜAlī himself approached the pavilion and took Aishah to task for the role she had played. She answered him with dignity and restraint, "You have conquered, show forbearance."[224] He did. He ordered her brother Mohammed to look after her, and the latter took her back to Baṣrah and put her up in the mansion of ᶜAbd Allah ibn Khalaf, whose household, like most of the tribes involved in this struggle,[225] had divided against itself, some to fight for Aishah and some for ᶜAlī.[226] Some of her followers, in-

[220] Ṭabarī, I, 3216 f. [221] Masᶜūdī, IV, 327; *ᶜIqd*, II, 267.

[222] Ibn Saᶜd, VIII, 44; cf. Ṭabarī, I, 3217; Tirmidhī, XIII, 259.

[223] Ṭabarī, I, 3217, 3232 f.; Ibn al-Athīr, III, 213; cf. Ibn Ḥanbal, IV, 58; Caetani, *op. cit.*, IX, 152.

[224] Ṭabarī, I, 3186; Ibn al-Athīr, III, 216; Yaᶜqūbī, II, 213; *ᶜIqd*, II, 282.

[225] Ṭabarī, I, 3182.

[226] *Ibid.*, pp. 3216, 3218, 3221, 3224 f.; cf. Ibn ᶜAsākir, VII, 65; *Aghānī*, XIX, 154.

cluding, according to some accounts, Marwān ibn al-Ḥakam, took refuge with her here.[227] She was so overjoyed to know that her beloved nephew, ᶜAbd Allah, was still alive that she gave the carrier of the happy news a royal purse.[228] ᶜAbd Allah got word to her of his hiding-place, and she ordered her brother Mohammed to bring him to her in safety.[229]

The detailed accounts of the events of the next few days emphasize ᶜAlī's great generosity toward the conquered foe.[230] They, for the most part, paint a very flattering picture of both ᶜAlī and Aishah. They minimize their long-standing animosity and present both as eager to bury the past and to start on a new road of friendship.[231] One source has it that Aishah even offered to stay with ᶜAlī and go with him on his campaigns against his enemy.[232] There can be little doubt, however, that this seemingly friendly attitude sprang not as much from the urging of the heart as from the dictates of reason and expediency. ᶜAlī would have probably lost some of the ground gained had he sought to wreak vengeance on the Mother of the Believers, now bereft of her candidates and leading supporters by death and desertion.[233] Aishah was

227 Ṭabarī, I, 3221; Ibn al-Athīr, III, 213; Masᶜūdī, IV, 331.

228 Ibn ᶜAsākir, VII, 402; *ᶜIqd*, I, 45.

229 Ṭabarī, I, 3221; Ibn al-Athīr, III, 213.

230 Ṭabarī, I, 3223–27; Masᶜūdī, IV, 331 f.; *ᶜIqd*, II, 279 f.; Ibn ᶜAsākir, VII, 86 f.

231 Ṭabarī, I, 3217, 3231.

232 Masᶜūdī, IV, 331.

233 Cf., e.g., *Kāmil*, p. 577.

practical enough to realize that her day of opposition and effective defiance was past. ᶜAlī, therefore, resorted only to mild threats when Aishah showed signs of resistance. While she, encountering firmness, sought first to parry her opponents with a show of temperament. But when this failed, she took the consequence of her defeat as gracefully as she knew how and left the field to the victor. How this actually worked is to be seen from the following incident, the details of which have probably been embellished by the original narrator, ᶜAbd Allah ibn al-ᶜAbbās, who, next to ᶜAlī and Aishah, was himself a chief actor in the story. After Aishah had been taken back to Baṣrah by her brother Mohammed, ᶜAlī sent ᶜAbd Allah to her with a message that she return to Medina. Aishah refused to receive ᶜAbd Allah, but he walked in and helped himself to a seat. She rebuked him for thus entering her house. He retorted that her house was at Medina, where she herself should have stayed. He then delivered ᶜAlī's message. She refused to listen and obey. ᶜAbd Allah did not mince his words. Aishah, though reduced to tears and seeing no way out of her unhappy position, still lashed her tormentor with her sharp tongue. "Yes, I will go," she cried out, "for a city in which you (plural) are is most hateful to me."[234]

ᶜAlī's dealings with her were, as already stated, more forbearing. He provided her with generous funds, equipped her handsomely for the return trip,

[234] ᶜ*Iqd*, II, 282; Yaᶜqūbī, II, 213; Masᶜūdī, IV, 330 f.

and sent a goodly escort of both men and women to accompany her on the return journey to Ḥijāz. When the day of departure arrived, ᶜAlī came in person to bid her goodbye. In a short farewell speech, Aishah once more rose to the demands of the occasion and bid her "sons" not to harbor hard feelings or seek to do harm one to another. By way of a needed example she assured them that there was never any personal hard feeling between her and ᶜAlī except such as usually arise between a woman and her in-laws. She went one step further and bore testimony to his goodness. ᶜAlī, in his turn, assured the crowd that she had indeed spoken the truth and gallantly upheld her position as Mother of the Believers by referring to her as "the wife of your prophet in this world and in the next."[235]

Traveling under the care of her brother Mohammed, Aishah left Baṣrah on Saturday, the first of Rajab, 36 (December 24, 656). She went to Mecca, where she remained for the annual pilgrimage, after which she returned to her home in Medina,[236] a disillusioned but wiser woman now in her early forties.

III

The question of Aishah's responsibility both for the murder of ᶜUthmān and for the civil war that followed is a lively one in Islamic records. Her recon-

[235] Ṭabarī, I, 3186 f., 3228, 3231; Masᶜūdī, IV, 334 f.; Yaᶜqūbī, II, 213.

[236] Ṭabarī, I, 2228, 3231; Masᶜūdī, IV, 334.

ciliation with ʿAlī and his party seems to have encouraged him and some of his leading men, as well as the later Shīʿite party, to place the blame for these evils not so much on Aishah herself as on her advisers, particularly the now dead Ṭalḥah and Zubair, with ʿAbd Allah too coming in for a good bit of this blame. ʿAlī himself led the way in this direction.[237] His peace envoy, Qaʿqāʿ, once the battle was over, consoled Aishah by calling her the best of Mothers but one that was not obeyed.[238] Ashtar, who denounced her nephew ʿAbd Allah and came near killing him in battle, followed his master's lead and made the friendly gesture of sending Aishah a costly camel to replace the fallen ʿAskar—a gift she could not bring herself to accept.[239] He and ʿAmmār called on Aishah in person sometime during this period. She took Ashtar to task for wishing to kill her nephew ʿAbd Allah and preached both men a neat sermon by telling them she had heard Mohammed say that only three acts called for the shedding of blood—adultery, apostasy, and murder.[240] ʿAbd Allah ibn al-ʿAbbās, who, as already seen, repeatedly crossed words with Aishah, now boldly told ʿAbd Allah ibn al-Zubair that it was he, his father, and his maternal uncle (Ṭalḥah) who led the Mother of the Believers to the civil war.[241] Even Muʿāwiyah, later as caliph, accused ʿAbd Allah and

[237] ʿ*Iqd*, II, 283; cf. *ibid.*, I, 336; Dīnawarī, p. 153.

[238] Ṭabarī, I, 3221.

[239] *Ibid.*, pp. 3200, 3227 f., 3162.

[240] Ibn Ḥanbal, VI, 58; Ibn Khallikān, IV, 536.

[241] ʿ*Iqd*, II, 137.

the Banū Zubair of deceiving Aishah.[242] Long after both ʿAlī and Aishah had gone to their rest, ʿAbd Allah ibn al-Zubair still had to face that accusation, this time at the hands of the Azāriqah Khārijites or "Seceders" who were debating about throwing in their lot with him as the rival caliph to the immediate successors of Muʿāwiyah. This group believed Aishah should have stayed home instead of going to war.[243] The sect, therefore, continued to censure her action, and one finds them in the third century of Islam cursing her publicly along with Ṭalḥah, Zubair, ʿAlī, and ʿUthmān.[244]

Saʿd ibn Abī Waqqāṣ, much-esteemed companion of the prophet, member of the council that elected ʿUthmān, and possible candidate for the caliphate in the event of ʿUthmān's deposition, was very much shocked at the murder of that caliph.[245] As he saw it, the ungodly deed was accomplished by a "sword drawn by Aishah, sharpened by Ṭalḥah, and poisoned by ʿAlī."[246] He deliberately refrained from taking the oath to ʿAlī until the latter was properly elected; and, having then taken the oath, he refused to join the rebels later against him.[247] He, therefore, took no part

[242] *Ibid.*, p, 139.

[243] *Ibid.*, I, 262 f.; *Kāmil*, pp. 606, 608.

[244] Ṭabarī, III, 1424; Ibn al-Athīr, VII, 52; Ibn Taghrībirdī, II, 49; cf. Kate Chambers Seelye, *Moslem Schisms and Sects* (New York, 1919), p. 115.

[245] Ṭabarī, I, 2969 f., 2998, 3019, 3072 f.; cf. ʿ*Iqd*, II, 267, 273; Ibn ʿAsākir, VI, 105.

[246] ʿ*Iqd*, II, 267.

[247] Ṭabarī, I, 3068, 2993; Masʿūdī, V, 43.

in either the Battle of the Camel or that of Ṣiffīn (37/657), which followed a few months after between the forces of ᶜAlī and Muᶜāwiyah. For the latter had decided to pick up the leadership in the fight for the blood of ᶜUthmān where the defeated Aishah had left it. At the ensuing and well-known arbitration ᶜAmr ibn al-ᶜĀṣ outwitted ᶜAlī's halfhearted and avowedly pacific representative, Abū Mūsā, who was led to set aside ᶜAlī as caliph and to suggest a new elective council.[248] This arbitration, though challenged and set aside by ᶜAlī, did nevertheless open up new possibilities for Muᶜāwiyah, who was now himself aspiring to the caliphate and who, therefore, sought to win over to his side as many of the leading men as he could reach. He wrote Saᶜd, urging him not to hold back from the ᶜUthmānic cause for which his associates Ṭalḥah and Zubair had worked and to which the Mother of the Believers had hastened. Saᶜd wrote back, pointing out that Muᶜāwiyah himself was not among those eligible for the caliphate while ᶜAlī was, that it would have been far better for Ṭalḥah and Zubair had they stayed home, and added that, as for the Mother of the Believers, may Allah forgive her for what she did.[249]

When Aishah met Mughīrah ibn Shuᶜbah, who, as stated above,[250] deserted her cause for a neutral path, she described to him how thick and fast the arrows came at her pavilion in the Battle of the Camel

[248] Cf. Wellhausen, *Arab Kingdom and Its Fall*, pp. 91–93.

[249] ᶜ*Iqd*, II, 286 f.; Yaᶜqūbī, II, 217.

[250] P. 143.

and how some of them pierced her skin. "Would to Allah," exclaimed he, "that some of them had killed you!"

"Allah have mercy upon you, why do you say that?" she asked.

"Perhaps it would have been an atonement for your slanders against ᶜUthmān."

"By Allah," came her answer, "you say that (because you suppose that) Allah knew I wished him killed. But Allah knew I wished for fighting, and I was fought against; (he knew) I wished for shooting, and I was shot at; (he knew) I wished for rebellion, and I was rebelled against. Now if Allah had indeed known that I wished him (ᶜUthmān) killed, I would have been killed."[251]

ᶜAmr ibn al-ᶜĀṣ, though he had his own grievances against ᶜUthmān and had watched with satisfaction Aishah's early stand against him, had shrewdly stepped into a neutral path of watchful waiting when matters reached the crisis of murder and civil war. He and Muᶜāwiyah got together against ᶜAlī *after* the Battle of the Camel.[252] It must have been during this period of active warfare and intensive political rivalry between ᶜAlī and Muᶜāwiyah that ᶜAmr said to Aishah, "I wish you had been killed in the Battle of the Camel." The puzzled Aishah asked the reason for his sentiment and was told, "You would then have

[251] ᶜ*Iqd*, II, 267; cf. Balādhurī, *Ansāb*, V, 101 f.

[252] Ṭabarī, I, 3249–54; Dīnawarī, pp. 167 f.; Yaᶜqūbī, II, 214–17; cf. Della Vida, "Il Califato ....," *op. cit.*, pp. 453 f.

died at the height of your glory and entered heaven, while we would have proclaimed your death as the most infamous act of ʿAlī."[253] In other words, ʿAmr was brazenly telling Aishah that she would have served the cause of Muʿāwiyah—and, therefore, that of ʿAmr himself—better dead than alive.

There are several traditions that make Aishah's own partisans, and even Aishah herself, accept the preceding versions of her responsibility and guilt for these events. There is, for instance, the statement that, when Mohammed ibn Ṭalḥah was asked to tell of the murder of ʿUthmān, he said that the responsibility for the blood of ʿUthmān goes in thirds: a third rests on her of the pavilion, meaning Aishah; a third on him of the red camel, meaning (his father) Ṭalḥah; and a third on ʿAlī.[254] There are several factors that stamp this tradition as a later fabrication of some ʿAlīd partisan. Mohammed's questioner is referred to as "a youth of Juhainah" who, on hearing Mohammed's reply, laughed and broke out into verse that ended with the line, "You have told the truth about the first two, but are mistaken about the radiant third," and then went on his way to join the forces of ʿAlī. Now Aishah's pavilion and Ṭalḥah's red mount first come to the fore in connection with the Battle of the Camel itself. It is, therefore, not likely that Mohammed, who lost his own life in the struggle around Aishah's camel, ever referred to Aishah and his own father as "she of the pavilion" and "he of the red

[253] *Kāmil*, p. 151.

[254] Ṭabarī, I, 3121.

camel," respectively. Again, terms of glowing praise were not associated with ᶜAlī until later in the development of the Shīᶜite party, so that Mohammed's questioner was not likely to refer to ᶜAlī as "radiant" or "shining." There is, furthermore, the consideration that Mohammed is generally represented as a pious and God-fearing man. He would, therefore, not have fought to the last in the cause of those he thus deemed guilty. The ᶜAlīd fabricator no doubt thought to give his statement more force, as far as Aishah and Ṭalḥah were concerned, by putting their condemnation in the mouth of one so God-fearing and so close to the accused culprits.

Again there is the tradition that credits Aishah with saying, "It was not because of my own judgment that I came out (on this war) with these."[255] She is said to have uttered the statement in the heat of the Battle of the Camel when she realized that her own followers were disunited and demoralized. If Aishah spoke such words at all, they could have had reference only to her actual participation in the battle; for, as already seen, it was Kaᶜb ibn Sūr who persuaded her to go into the fighting lines in the hope of averting a major engagement.

Regardless of what judgment friend or foe passed on Aishah's guilt in connection with the murder of ᶜUthmān, and despite their efforts to free her of the main responsibility for the rebellion and civil war that followed, she herself, as stated before, repeatedly

[255] ᶜ*Iqd*, I, 37; cf. *ibid.*, p. 336; Masᶜūdī, IV, 335.

and vigorously denied any guilt for the former but bravely shouldered her share of the responsibility for the latter. Her answer to Mughīrah stated emphatically the position she took on both questions, but it said nothing as to her motives. Her primary motive was, she insisted on many an occasion, the setting of things right among the Moslems—a motive that she claimed was operative both in her criticism of ᶜUthmān and in her rebellion against ᶜAlī. Did they then think, she once argued for the benefit of some bewildered and reluctant Baṣrans, that she who had censured ᶜUthmān for his misdeeds would overlook the greater misdeeds of his murderers?[256] The fact that she hoped at the same time to raise one of her clan to the caliphate does not necessarily belie her avowed motive. Just as there were those of her own day and time who approved her action and accepted her motive, so too there were those of later centuries who thought of following her example[257] and others who continued to defend the sincerity of her avowed motive.[258]

Aishah was much too practical to need anyone like ᶜAmr ibn al-ᶜĀṣ to point out to her that her defeat at the Battle of the Camel marked the turning-point of her political career. She, therefore, for more than one reason looked back with regret on this phase of her life. Her undertaking, no matter how sincere and jus-

[256] Ṭabarī, I, 3159. [257] Masᶜūdī, VI, 485.

[258] Tirmidhī, XIII, 254 f., marginal commentary of Ibn al-ᶜArabī (d. 543/1148).

tified in her own estimation, had failed miserably. It had led to the shedding of much Moslem blood, to the death of some of her nearest and dearest, and to the loss of much of her own prestige.[259] It is no wonder then that she herself at times wished she had died not at the Battle of the Camel but twenty years earlier[260] or that she wept when reciting the Qurʾānic verses, "O wives of the Prophet . . . . remain in your houses."[261] There are those who credit this childless widow of Mohammed with saying, "It would be more to my liking had I remained in my house and not gone on my expedition to Baṣrah than to have borne ten noble and heroic sons to Mohammed."[262]

Most of the reasons for the failure of Aishah's bold undertaking have been touched upon in the course of this narrative. She could not overcome the age-long practice of tribes and subtribes to feel out any given situation to their own best advantage. She had not the wholehearted support of the two leading Umayyads, Marwān and Muʿāwiyah, who, under the circumstances, should have assumed more active responsibility for a movement that claimed to avenge the blood of ʿUthmān. Closer home she had rival candidates for leadership in the persons of Ṭalḥah and Zubair, at the same time that she had an openly divided family with her brother Mohammed counted by many among the regicides and fighting against her

[259] Ṭabarī, I, 3197, 3201; Masʿūdī, IV, 333 f.

[260] Ṭabarī, I, 3221 f., 3236; Balādhurī, *Ansāb*, V, 101.

[261] Sūrah 33:22 f.; cf. Ibn Saʿd, VIII, 56.

[262] Ibn Saʿd, V, 1.

in the camp of ᶜAlī. Her favorite and beloved nephew, ᶜAbd Allah ibn al-Zubair, was more a man after her own heart and one that had his whole heart in the undertaking. But the prestige that had grown around the first Companions of the prophet and the members of the elective council made it impossible for Aishah to set him up for leadership ahead of his father Zubair and relative Ṭalḥah, on the one hand, and in opposition to ᶜAlī, on the other.

But over and above these reasons, Aishah's failure is to be attributed in some measure to the fact of her sex. Notwithstanding her driving personal ambition, great political energy, and marked ability for organization and propaganda, she could hardly be expected to escape the fate of the Quraishite Hind and the Tamīmite Sajāḥ, both of whom suffered political defeat something like a quarter of a century earlier.[263] For, in addition to such obstacles as these two enterprising women had to face in their day of transition from pre-Islamic to Islamic times, Aishah was further handicapped with the institution of seclusion introduced at the start in connection with Mohammed's harem and reinforced by the Qurʾānic injunction ordering the wives of the prophet to keep to their homes.[264] These new and powerful weapons were used against her repeatedly and forcefully by her oppo-

[263] See Abbott, "Women and the State on the Eve of Islam," *op. cit.*, pp. 269–78, 281–84.

[264] Surāh 33:33; cf. above, pp. 20–26 and 57.

nents, so that in some respects they more than counteracted the advantages derived from the fact of her being the Mother of the Believers. Her party, both before and after the Battle of the Camel, was taunted with the fact that it was a "party headed by a woman."[265] After her defeat in battle one of her own mortally wounded followers bewailed the fact that he had been "deceived by a woman who wished to be the Commander of the Believers."[266]

So deep rooted and determined was this antipathy of some of the faithful to the rule and leadership of a woman that soon someone was found ready to assert that Mohammed himself had deplored the government of a people by a woman. The tradition, though appearing mostly in slightly different versions, is nevertheless a singleton, since it seems to be always traced back to the one man, Abū Bakrah. This Abū Bakrah is most probably the freedman of Mohammed, Nafīᶜ ibn Masrūḥ, known to have transmitted traditions from Mohammed.[267] He claimed that Allah delivered him from joining Aishah's forces when she came to Baṣrah by recalling to his mind a statement of Mohammed. The latter, it seems, having just heard that a princess had been raised to the Persian throne,[268] remarked, "No people who place a

[265] Ṭabarī, I, 3185; ᶜ*Iqd*, II, 169 f., 137; cf. also Yāqūt, I, 646 f.

[266] Masᶜūdī, IV, 333 f.

[267] Ibn Saᶜd, II¹, 114 f.; *Iṣābah*, III, 1178, No. 8303; IV, 39.

[268] Cf. Ibn al-Athī., I, 363–65; Caetani, *op. cit.*, II¹, 304.

woman over their affairs prosper."[269] One version, though it too is traced back to Abū Bakrah, differs considerably from the rest in that it makes Mohammed repeat thrice, "The men perish if they obey the women."[270] An effort is elsewhere made to show that Mohammed, who took the advice of his wives Khadījah and Umm Salamah and who referred in the Qurʾān to the good government of the Queen of Sheba, was not likely to utter such sentiments.[271] The tradition, nevertheless, gained such wide acceptance that it came in time to be used as the basis of all major political discrimination against the Moslem woman.[272]

Such, then, was the intensely human and definitely complex situation that ended finally in Aishah's military and political defeat. Despite this complete failure, the spirited Aishah still continued, for something like a quarter of a century, to exercise her personal influence on the Moslem state and community. But that is the theme of the next chapter.

[269] Bukhārī, IV, 376 f.; Ibn Ḥanbal, V, 38 f., 43, 47, 50, 51; Nasāʾī, *Sunan* (Cairo, 1894), II, 305; Tirmidhī, *Sahīh*, IX, 118 f.

[270] Ibn Ḥanbal, V, 45.

[271] See Abbott, "Women and the State in Early Islam," *op. cit.*, 121–24.

[272] Cf. Māwardī, *Kitāb al-Aḥkām al-Sulṭānīyah* (Cairo, A.H. 1298), p. 26.

III

Sage and Saint in Islam

I

THOUGH Aishah had made her peace with ʿAlī and retired from front-rank participation in the field of politics, yet Muʿāwiyah continued to keep in touch with her and to use her past revolt as an argument for his cause. Aishah herself, who could hardly be indifferent to the continuation of the civil war, now between Muʿāwiyah and ʿAlī, seems nevertheless to have striven for at least an outward show of neutrality. Muʿāwiyah saw fit to send her a special messenger, Zufar ibn Ḥārith, with news of the Battle of Ṣiffīn (A.H. 37/A.D. 657).[1] One suspects that neither the details nor the real purpose of this message are recorded, since it is not likely that Muʿāwiyah would be any too anxious to report the near-defeat of his Syrian army in that engagement—a defeat averted only by the timely ruse of raising the Qurʾān on his soldiers' spearheads and appealing to the Book to decide between the warring parties. Did Muʿāwiyah hope to use Aishah directly or indirectly

[1] Ibn ʿAsākir, *Tārīkh al-Kabīr* (Damascus, 1329——/1911——), V, 376.

in the arbitration that was to follow, or was he merely trying to keep her from actively aiding ʿAlī? Did not Aishah, deep in her heart, feel that Muʿāwiyah was, by reason of the lone hand he had played, in part at least responsible for her defeat and consequent loss of prestige? What, then, was likely to have been her real reaction to the news of the Battle of Ṣiffīn? One can only speculate on the answers to these questions. The records themselves say nothing except that Zufar reported the death of some of the fallen, including that of her erstwhile opponent and ʿAlī's right-hand man, ʿAmmār ibn Yāsir, for whom she now had a word of praise.

Again there is no record of Aishah's reaction to the arbitration that followed when Abū Mūsā, representing the cause of ʿAlī, was outwitted by ʿAmr ibn al-ʿĀṣ. However, the reaction of her brother, ʿAbd al-Raḥmān, may reflect her attitude, for the two generally supported each other in their politics and public expressions. ʿAbd al-Raḥmān, and Aishah too for that matter, knew full well that it was the caliphate and not just revenge for ʿUthmān's blood that Muʿāwiyah, aided by ʿAmr, was after. ʿAbd al-Raḥmān was thus not only suspicious of the motives behind the arbitration but also critical of its procedure and is reported as saying, "Had (Abū Mūsā) al-Ashʿarī died before this, it would have been better for him."[2]

[2] Ibn Saʿd, *Ṭabaqāt* (9 vols.; Leiden, 1905–40), IV, 5; Ṭabarī, *Tārīkh* ("Annales"), ed. de Goeje (15 vols.; Lugduni Batavorum, 1879–1901), II, 84.

Abū Mūsā's wished-for death might have been better also for the children of Abū Bakr. For the great ambitions and carefully laid plans of Muᶜāwiyah and ᶜAmr soon cost Mohammed ibn Abū Bakr his life, a loss which brought both sorrow and humiliation to Aishah and ᶜAbd al-Raḥmān. Mohammed had at last received the reward for his efforts in ᶜAlī's cause when the latter had appointed him to the rich and much-coveted governorship of Egypt.[3] It was this same governorship that ᶜAmr had bargained for with Muᶜāwiyah. He now lost no time in setting out to acquire it. In the ensuing military struggle the inexperienced Mohammed, facing discontent in his own province, came out second best. Defeated on the field, he fled into hiding. He was discovered and brought before ᶜAmr and his lieutenant Muᶜāwiyah ibn Ḥudaij.[4] This latter is generally credited with dispatching the now helpless but still defiant Mohammed to his final rest and with justifying his deed as retaliation for the part Mohammed had played in the murder of ᶜUthmān. ᶜAbd al-Raḥmān, sent by Aishah to ᶜAmr on behalf of her brother, appealed to the latter to save Mohammed's life. ᶜAmr tried to restrain Muᶜāwiyah ibn Ḥudaij, but the latter paid no

[3] Ṭabarī, I, 3245–48; Kindī, *Kitāb al-Wulāh wa-Kitāb al-Quḍah* ("Governors and Judges of Egypt"), ed. R. Guest (Leiden and London, 1912), pp. 26–31; Ibn Taghrībirdī, *Nujūm . . . .* ("Annals"), ed. W. Popper (Berkeley, Calif., 1909——), I, 120–28; cf. Della Vida, "Il Califato di Ali secondo il *Katāb Ansāb al-Aŝrāf* di al-Balāḍurā," *Revista degli studi orientali*, VI (1913–15), 498–503.

[4] Ṭabarī, I, 3390–3407.

heed to him.[5] The method of execution was barbaric. Having first threatened to place Mohammed in the skin of an ass and then roast him to death, Muʿāwiyah lost his temper with him and killed him on the spot. Nevertheless, neither Muʿāwiyah's vengeance nor his wrath was satisfied until he had the corpse wrapped in an ass's skin and burned.[6]

The defeat and murder of Mohammed (Ṣafar, 38/July–August, 658) meant that ʿAmr was once more in possession of his beloved Egypt and Muʿāwiyah ahead of his opponent ʿAlī. To Mohammed's own party and to the different members of his family his death brought consternation and grief. ʿAlī realized full well the significance of his enemy's victory in the rich province of Egypt, coming, as it did, so soon after the mysterious death of his general Ashtar, who was on his way to relieve Mohammed of his Egyptian governorship. He grieved over both men but mourned especially the death of his "son" Mohammed.[7] Mohammed's mother, Asmā, who was then one of ʿAlī's wives, mourned him excessively.[8] When Aishah herself heard of the murder, she gave vent to her grief and wrath by calling down curses on his

[5] Ṭabarī, I, 3405; *ibid.*, II, 84; Ibn Taghrībirdī, I, 125; Damirī, *Ḥayāt-al-Ḥayawān* (Cairo, 1881), I, 343.

[6] Ṭabarī, I, 3405 f.

[7] Yaʿqūbī, *Tārīkh*, ed. Houtsma (2 vols.; Lugduni Batavorum, 1883), II, 227.

[8] Kindī, p. 31; Ibn Ḥajar, *Kitāb al-Iṣābah* (Calcutta, 1873), IV, 439.

murderers, Muʿāwiyah and ʿAmr.[9] The text does not specify whether it was Muʿāwiyah ibn Abī Sufyān, as Lammens seems to think,[10] or Muʿāwiyah ibn Ḥudaij, the actual murderer of Mohammed, that was thus cursed by Aishah, though she was not incapable of including both.[11] That she for some time harbored strong resentment against the former is brought out in the following incident. Muʿāwiyah seems to have considered it worth while to call on Aishah in person while on his pilgrimage trips. He led the annual pilgrimages of the Years 44 and 50 or 51 and made the lesser pilgrimage in 56.[12] It was most probably during his visit to her in the first of these three years that Aishah asked him if he were not afraid to enter her house lest she have him assassinated in revenge for the murder of her brother. Ibn al-Athīr places the episode in 56,[13] which is highly improbable, since, as we shall see, Aishah and Muʿāwiyah had found out how to get along with each other long before that date.

[9] Ṭabarī, I, 3406; Ibn al-Athīr, *Al-Kāmil fī al-Tārīkh* ("Chronicon"), ed. C. J. Torneberg (14 vols.; Lugduni Batavorum, 1851–76), III, 300; cf. Abū Zakariyā Yaḥyā al-Nawawī, *Kitāb Tahdhīb al-Asmā*, ed. Wüstenfeld (Göttingen, 1842–47), p. 110.

[10] "Moʿâwia Ier," *MOFB*, II (1907), 3 f., n. 8.

[11] Cf. Ṭabarī, II, 145; Ibn al-Athīr, III, 422.

[12] Yaʿqūbī, II, 283; Masʿūdī, *Murūj al-Dhahab*, ed. C. Barbier de Meynard (9 vols.; Paris, 1861–77), IX, 57; Ṭabarī, II, 94, 156.

[13] Ibn al-Athīr, III, 422; cf. Ṭabarī, II, 145, where it is associated with the second of these annual pilgrimages, but where it is obviously out of context.

Aishah, however, was not permitted to mourn her departed brother in dignified and undisturbed grief. Umm Ḥabībah, Umayyad Mother of the Believers, and Nāʾilah, widow of ʿUthmān, both had good reasons to hate the children of Abū Bakr. The one had been Aishah's old harem rival and her opponent in defense of ʿUthmān; the other held Mohammed responsible for the murder of her husband. The two, therefore, celebrated the death of Mohammed in a manner suggested by his barbarous murder. They roasted a ram and sent it to Aishah with the heartless message, "So was your brother roasted." Aishah, adds the historian, "could eat no more roasted meat for the rest of her life."[14]

Whatever her real feelings toward either ʿAlī or Muʿāwiyah, Aishah kept her peace with ʿAlī for as long as he lived. Once when asked about the prophet's practice or regulations on ritualistic washing, she sent the inquirer to ʿAlī, saying the latter was better informed than she was on that subject.[15] The time of the incident is not specified, but this is obviously the most probable period for it. When news of ʿAlī's murder (Ramadān, 40/January, 661) was received in Medina, Aishah's grief and her public mourning for him surprised and convinced her onlookers. She is said to have stood at the tomb of Mohammed and there in the presence of the crowd and in the intensity of her grief she tearfully enumerated many of ʿAlī's excel-

[14] Kindī, p. 30; Ibn al-Athīr, III, 300.

[15] Ibn Ḥanbal, *Musnad* (6 vols.; Cairo, 1313/1895–96), I, 113.

lent qualities, emphasizing the ties of blood and bonds of affection that had existed between the prophet and his cousin and son-in-law. Though the phraseology of this speech has the earmarks of Shīʿite enthusiasm, it is nevertheless possible that it was based on some public demonstration on Aishah's part.[16] Ṭabarī's report of her first reaction to the news would seem to indicate a sense of relief on her part, though one that she did not wish to express publicly.[17]

The death of ʿAlī and the subsequent terms between his son Ḥasan and Muʿāwiyah, which left the latter sole and undisputed caliph of Islam (41/661), induced no less an ʿAlīd figure than ʿAbd Allah ibn al-ʿAbbās to come to an understanding with Muʿāwiyah and his Umayyads—an understanding that netted ʿAbd Allah an enormous sum of money from the Baṣran treasury.[18] Aishah's recognition of Muʿāwiyah called for no such party desertion. She had been among the first to raise the cry for the blood of ʿUthmān, and that cry had played a major propagandistic role in raising Muʿāwiyah to the caliphate as heir and avenger of his slain kinsman. Nevertheless, Muʿāwiyah, with his keen knowledge of human nature, did not expect any enthusiastic support of his cause or unquestioned compliance with his deeds from this Mother of the Believers whose personal

[16] Ibn ʿAbd Rabbihi, *ʿIqd al-Farīd* (3 vols.; Cairo, 1293/1876), I, 382 f.

[17] Ṭabarī, I, 3466; Ibn al-Athīr, III, 331.

[18] Cf. Wellhausen, *The Arab Kingdom and Its Fall*, trans. Margaret Graham Weir (Calcutta, 1927), pp. 104–12.

losses in this brief period of five or six years proved to be in inverse proportion to his own great successes. Neither was he one to underestimate her understanding of the political situation and her ability to disturb it. The statesman in him led him to court her friendship and approval now by a royal gift or a flattering request for information or again by granting her a request or seeming to heed her rebuke.

On her part Aishah, too, knew how to time her favors and realized just how far she could go in this give-and-take game with the masterly Muᶜāwiyah. Not the least effective of her tools in this conditioned co-operation was her generally recognized eloquence. Muᶜāwiyah once asked his half-brother Ziyād to name the most eloquent person he knew. "You, O Commander of the Believers," answered Ziyād. But Muᶜāwiyah, who knew his talents ran in other direction, was not to be so easily flattered and put off. He insisted that Ziyād express his real opinion. "Since you insist," said Ziyād, "then (I say) it is Aishah." To which Muᶜāwiyah replied, "I never yet opened a subject she wished closed but that she closed it, nor closed I a subject she wished opened but that she opened it."[19]

It is not always possible to determine the occasion or the amount of the gifts that Muᶜāwiyah presented to Aishah; nor is it likely that the few recorded in-

[19] Ibn al-Jauzī, *Ṣifat al-Ṣafwah* (4 vols.; Ḥaidarābād, 1936–37), II, 18; cf. Abū al-Faraj al-Iṣbahānī, *Kitāb al-Aghānī* (20 vols.; Cairo, 1285/1868), XXI, 14 f.

stances of such political gifts present a complete picture of this phase of their relationships. One reads of one or two instances when Muᶜāwiyah sent her large sums of money all or part of which she, in turn, is said to have given away.[20] Sometimes his gifts took the form of fine clothes or of expensive jewelry, some of which she seems to have shared with her "sisters."[21] She, too, had gifts, though of a different nature, to make to Muᶜāwiyah, to whom she once sent a tunic of the prophet.[22]

Far more valuable to Muᶜāwiyah than even such an honored relic was her share of propaganda in the establishment of the ᶜUthmānic legend which bore so directly on Muᶜāwiyah's efforts to justify his right to the caliphate as the heir of ᶜUthmān. Aishah's contributions in this direction had both a negative and a positive phase—negative in that she chose to ignore ᶜAlī's relationships to Mohammed, especially where the question of succession was involved, and positive in that she dwelt on such relationships between Mohammed and ᶜUthmān. The traditions record an instructive instance of the latter type. Nuᶜmān ibn Bashīr was active in the ᶜUthmānic cause and in high favor with Muᶜāwiyah. It was he who had brought Nāʾilah's message to Muᶜāwiyah after the murder of

[20] Abū Nuᶜaim, *Ḥilyat al-Awlīyā* . . . . (10 vols.; Cairo, 1932–38), II, 47; but see also *ibid.*, p. 49; Ibn Saᶜd, V, 18.

[21] Abū Nuᶜaim, II, 48; *Ṣifat al-Ṣafwah*, II, 13 f.

[22] Cf. Lammens, "Le 'Triumvirat' ...," *MFOB*, IV (1910), 121 f., n. 7.

ᶜUthmān. He was with Muᶜāwiyah at the Battle of Ṣiffīn. When hostilities were again resumed after the failure of the famous arbitration, Nuᶜmān was doing his share of the fighting against ᶜAlī.[23] Muᶜāwiyah once sent a message with this Nuᶜmān to Aishah. The message itself is unrecorded. However, in the course of the conversation Aishah told Nuᶜmān that Mohammed had definitely instructed ᶜUthmān not to resign from an office to be bestowed on him by Allah. Asked why she had not mentioned this before, she replied that she had so completely forgotten it that it never occurred to her that she had heard it. Nuᶜmān reported the conversation to Muᶜāwiyah, who wrote Aishah asking her to put it down in black and white for him, which she did.[24]

The above incident is illustrative of how traditions frequently came to be attributed to Mohammed in order to forward some later political cause. In the present instance the significant conversation between ᶜUthmān and Mohammed is obviously a fabrication. The only question is by whom and when it was fabricated. There are two possibilities: either it was originated by the Umayyads *after* the death of Aishah or it was invented by Aishah herself in co-operation with Muᶜāwiyah. The latter seems the more probable since it would put the tradition into circulation at a time when it could be used to the best positive advantage.

[23] Ṭabarī, I, 3070, 3255, 3444 f.

[24] Ibn Ḥanbal, VI, 86 f., 149. For different accounts of Mohammed's interview(s) with ᶜUthmān see *ibid.*, pp. 52, 63, 75, 114, 214 f., 263.

As far as Aishah's own interests were concerned, this post-ᶜAlīd period would seem to be the best time to recall such a tradition. It would not do for her to remember it when she herself was calling for ᶜUthmān's deposition and when that caliph repeatedly refused "to resign an office bestowed on him by Allah," using almost the very words attributed to Mohammed.[25] She did not use the tradition during her own period of active revolt against ᶜAlī, and it is not likely she would bring it forward in the interval between her defeat and the death of ᶜAlī for the sole use and benefit of Muᶜāwiyah. So the tradition continued to be "completely forgotten" until this time when it could be used in this give-and-take game between her and the now successful and powerful Muᶜāwiyah.

It was during this period, too, that one day the now reconciled ᶜAbd Allah ibn al-ᶜAbbās, seeing the people perform prayers at an odd hour in the day, came to Muᶜāwiyah and asked for an explanation, protesting at the same time that he had never seen the prophet either perform that prayer or command it. Muᶜāwiyah informed him that it was performed on the authority of (ᶜAbd Allah) Ibn al-Zubair. Presently Ibn al-Zubair came in and was faced with the question, whereupon he claimed that Aishah, the Mother of the Believers, had informed him that Mohammed had performed that prayer in her house. To settle the controversy, Muᶜāwiyah sent two messengers to Aishah to ascertain the facts. Her answer came back

[25] E.g., Ṭabarī, I, 2997, 2989.

that she had been told of the prayer by Umm Salamah and that Ibn al-Zubair did not remember well; for, though she had indeed told him that the Messenger of Allah had performed that prayer, she had also added that it was in continuation of an earlier and regular prayer of the day that had been disturbed.[26]

ᶜAbd Allah ibn al-Zubair and some member of ᶜAlī's family clashed on more than one occasion in the court and presence of Muᶜāwiyah. Once he and Ḥasan ibn ᶜAlī rehashed afresh the feud and civil war between ᶜAlī, on the one hand, and Aishah, Ṭalḥah, and Zubair, on the other. Abū Saᶜīd, a nephew of ᶜAlī, joined in the verbal fight, and among other taunts and accusations belittled the Zubairid cause as one headed by a woman. The news was carried to Aishah; how and by whom is not told. When Abū Saᶜīd next passed by her place, she cried out to him and berated him roundly for saying thus and so to her nephew. Abū Saᶜīd, however, was equal to holding his own with her by some clever repartee which caused her to laugh off the episode.[27]

Aishah had a certain mastery of technique that at times enabled her to accomplish more than one objective with a well-timed act. Muᶜāwiyah had, for very good political reasons, decided early in his reign (44/664) to acknowledge the legitimacy of Ziyād ibn Abīhi or "Ziyād the son of his father," who was suspected of being a natural son of Abū Sufyān and,

[26] Ibn Ḥanbal, VI, 183 f., 303, 311.

[27] ᶜ*Iqd*, II, 137.

therefore, half-brother to Muᶜāwiyah. The act was a daring one, since it cast reflections on Abū Sufyān's character. Muᶜāwiyah and Ziyād had to consider ways and means of reconciling other members of the family—including their half-sister Umm Ḥabībah, widow of Mohammed—to the accomplished act.[28] Umayyads and non-Umayyads alike were shocked, and some refused to follow Muᶜāwiyah's lead. Among the latter was Aishah's brother, ᶜAbd al-Raḥmān. His freedman, Murrah, who had been first captured at Baṣrah, coveted some favor from Ziyād, who had been appointed by Muᶜāwiyah to the governorship of Baṣrah. He requested ᶜAbd al-Raḥmān to write Ziyād on his behalf. ᶜAbd al-Raḥmān complied but did not address his letter "To Ziyād ibn Abī Sufyān." Murrah realized that a letter without this address would do his cause more harm than good, and so he would not use it. He took his case to Aishah, who had hitherto guardedly yet pointedly addressed her letters to Ziyād: "From Aishah, Mother of the Believers, to her son Ziyād."[29] But she now rose to the occasion, wrote the letter, and addressed it "To Ziyād ibn Abī Sufyān." When Murrah presented himself and the letter, Ziyād was delighted with the form of address, the significance of which was fully appreciated by him. He proceeded to make the most of it. He treated Murrah graciously and asked that

[28] Yaᶜqūbī, II, 273; Ibn Khallikān, *Biographical Dictionary*, trans. W. M. de Slane (4 vols.; Paris, 1843–71), IV, 249; Ibn al-Athīr, III, 369–72.

[29] Ibn al-Athīr, III, 372.

he read the address aloud before the assembled people. He thus published the fact that Aishah, Mother of the Believers, had acknowledged his legitimacy. In return for so gracious a deed Ziyād was only too happy to present this freedman of Abū Bakr's family with a grant of land in Baṣrah.[30] So did Aishah score three points with one stroke.

There are sufficient indications that there was frequent correspondence between Aishah and Muᶜāwiyah, though again the when and why of such correspondence is not always indicated. We read, for instance, that she wrote him: "When a man does what is hateful to Allah, those among the people who had first praised him will then reproach him. Goodbye."[31] Just what called forth this note of warning from Aishah to Muᶜāwiyah is not stated. It may and may not have been connected with the following episode.

The Kindite Ḥujr ibn ᶜAdī[32] had been among the Kūfans who had protested Saᶜīd's government of that city to ᶜUthmān and who had continued thereafter to be active in the opposition to ᶜUthmān and high in the service and counsel of ᶜAlī, to whose cause he was wholeheartedly devoted. With the triumph of Muᶜāwiyah, the position of Ḥujr and those of similar persuasion was not any too comfortable. Many, un-

[30] Ibn Saᶜd, VII¹, 71; Balādhurī, *Futūḥ al-Buldān*, ed. de Goeje (Lugduni Batavorum, 1886), pp. 360 f.

[31] *ᶜIqd*, I, 24; *Ṣifat al-Ṣafwah*, II, 15.

[32] Ṭabarī, II, 111–55; Ibn al-Athīr, III, 392–408; Ibn Saᶜd, VI, 152 f.; *Aghānī*, XVI, 2–11.

der the new circumstances, compromised with the powers that were, and not a few went over to the victorious party. Among the latter was Ziyād ibn Abīhi, who switched over from ᶜAlī's now leaderless faction to become Ziyād ibn Abī Sufyān in Muᶜāwiyah's political camp. Not so Ziyād's former political companion and friend, Ḥujr. Mughīrah, Muᶜāwiyah's governor of Kūfah, was not anxious to make matters pleasant for the Shīᶜah, or party of ᶜAlī. Ḥujr, who soon came to be considered as the leader of this party, protested the injustice of the new regime's discrimination against his group and proceeded to stir up trouble in Kūfah. His rivals and enemies appealed to the aged Mughīrah, who, now that he felt his own end approaching, preferred to let the blood of Ḥujr and his friends rest on the shoulders of his successor in office. That successor was, ironically enough, Ḥujr's old friend Ziyād.

No sooner did Ziyād take over the governorship of Kūfah than he tackled the affair of Ḥujr. He called him into his presence and gave him a friendly warning. All his great former love for ᶜAlī, he now told Ḥujr, had turned to hate, as all his former hate for Muᶜāwiyah had turned into love. He dwelt on their past friendship, which, he said, he wished to see continued, provided Ḥujr ceased from his activities. Ḥujr promised not to cause Ziyād any anxiety. But Ziyād, being governor of both Kūfah and Baṣrah, divided his time between the two provinces, appointing a deputy-governor for each for the periods of his absence. It was in Ziyād's absence that Ḥujr seems to have grown more indignant at the treatment of the Shīʿah and bolder in denouncing the ʿUthmānid-Umayyad regime. He soon won so considerable a following that Ziyād, fearing a major revolt in the making, decided to strike quickly. After some rioting and fighting, Ḥujr was taken prisoner, and pressure was again brought to bear on him to retract his ʿAlīd allegiance and sever connections with the Shīʿah. Ḥujr refused. Meanwhile, Muʿāwiyah, who was kept informed of the situation, ordered Ḥujr and his leading supporters sent to him in Syria. For some time Muʿāwiyah could not decide between killing or pardoning his prisoners, not being quite sure which alternative would serve his cause best. He wrote Ziyād of this. Ziyād wrote back that under no circumstances did he wish the prisoners returned to Kūfah, and again he urged Muʿāwiyah to execute them, which Muʿāwiyah eventually did.

As far as Aishah was concerned, this disturbance in the Moslem empire had several features similar to those of the provincial troubles in the time of ʿUthmān. Aishah's own position, however, had changed. That change is reflected in her reactions to the newer situation. She felt herself strong enough to address a plea to Muʿāwiyah on behalf of the culprits, but her letter reached Muʿāwiyah too late.[33] When she heard of the mass execution of Ḥujr and at least six of his leading companions, she did not feel herself in a posi-

[33] Ṭabarī, II, 145; Ibn Saʿd, VI, 152 f.; *Aghānī*, XVI, 11.

tion to do anything positive about it. Her reaction is reported as follows: "Were it not that we altered nothing but that matters lead us into a worse condition than that in which we were before, we would surely demand blood-price for the murder of Ḥujr. So far as I know, he was a (good) Moslem observing the Ḥajj and the ᶜ*Umrah* (the greater and lesser pilgrimage)."[34] The date of the execution is variously given from A.H. 50 to 53,[35] though several factors point to either 50 or 51. Ziyād, who became governor of Baṣrah in 50, lost no time in getting rid of Ḥujr. It was on Muᶜāwiyah's second pilgrimage, which took place in either 50 or 51, that Aishah took him to task with, "O Muᶜāwiyah, did you not fear Allah in the killing of Ḥujr and his companions?"

"It was not I who killed them," said Muᶜāwiyah, "but those who bore witness against them," or "I had no man with me rightly guided."[36] The historians frequently add that Muᶜāwiyah blamed Ziyād for this deed, which he regretted until the end of his days.[37]

Muᶜāwiyah, during the last decade of his reign, was particularly active in securing the succession for his son Yazīd. At first he prepared the ground carefully and secretly until enough of his friends and followers could be relied upon to support the move in public. He had to overcome opposition to the scheme from

34 See preceding references to Ṭabarī and *Aghānī*.

35 Masᶜūdī, V, 15–17; Yaᶜqūbī, II, 275, 283.

36 Ṭabarī, II, 145, 116; Yaᶜqūbī, II, 275.

37 Ṭabarī, II, 116 f., 146; *Aghānī*, XVI, 11.

among other branches of the Umayyads, Marwān ibn al-Ḥakam being among the first to protest,[38] though he was eventually won over. But the group that Muᶜāwiyah strove the hardest either to intimidate or to persuade were the second generation of Moslems who, through their connection with Mohammed, the first four caliphs, and the members of the elective council, considered themselves or were considered by the Moslems as true candidates for the caliphate. Among these were ᶜAbd al-Raḥmān ibn Abī Bakr, Ḥusain ibn ᶜAlī, and the three ᶜAbd Allahs—ᶜAbd allah ibn ᶜUmar, ᶜAbd Allah ibn al-ᶜAbbās, and ᶜAbd Allah ibn al-Zubair.[39] Aishah would naturally be interested in the prospects and reactions of the first and the last mentioned, these being her full brother and favorite nephew, respectively, both of whom had shared her defeat at the Battle of the Camel. However, there is no record of any attempt on her part to take the initiative in their cause, though both were outspoken in their opposition to Yazīd's nomination.

ᶜAbd al-Raḥmān refused to fall in line when Marwān, as Muᶜāwiyah's governor of Medina, called the people of Ḥijāz to take the oath of allegiance to Yazīd as heir. He went further and contrasted Muᶜāwiyah's move with that of his own father, Abū Bakr, who had passed over his sons and appointed

[38] Masᶜūdī, V, 69–73; *Aghānī*, XII, 72–74; XVIII, 71; cf. Lammens, "Le Califat de Yazīd I," *BMFO*, V (1912), 96–104.

[39] Ṭabarī, II, 175 f., 196 f.; ᶜ*Iqd*, II, 303; but see Wellhausen, *op. cit.*, p. 144.

ᶜUmar as his successor. He accused Muᶜāwiyah of trying to establish dynasties like the Byzantines and the Persians, who pass the succession from father to son. Marwān, seeking to discredit ᶜAbd al-Raḥmān by casting reflections on his lack of both faith and filial respect, cried out that this was he of whom it was revealed: But he who had said to his parents, "Fie upon you! Do you promise me that I shall be brought out (of the grave) though the generations before me have passed away?"[40] This was too much for Aishah. She cried out loudly to Marwān: "Do you indeed say this of ᶜAbd al-Raḥmān? By Allah, you lie! The verse does not refer to him. If you wish me to name the person to whom the verse refers, I will surely name him. But I bear witness that I heard the Messenger of Allah curse your father while you were yet in his loins; so that you yourself are included in the curse of Allah." She was seemingly not content with this outburst, for she is reported to have threatened to make a public attack on him on Friday (when the mosque crowds are the largest). Marwān was alarmed and later sought to pacify her with his apologies, vowing that he would not lead in prayers until she promised not to attack him, which promise he eventually secured.[41]

Later when in 56/675 Muᶜāwiyah himself came to

[40] Sūrah 46:16; cf. Richard Bell, *The Qurʾān* (Edinburgh, 1939), II, 509 f.

[41] ᶜ*Iqd*, II, 303; *Aghānī*, XVI, 94; Ibn al-Athīr, III, 419 f.; *Iṣābah*, II, 979 f.

Medina to work on the question of Yazīd's succession, he is said to have attempted in vain to bribe ᶜAbd al-Raḥmān.[42] Even then Muᶜāwiyah knew him to be in reality the least dangerous of his son's opponents, since ᶜAbd al-Raḥmān's reputation as a pleasure-loving lady's man had not escaped the shrewd caliph.[43] Nevertheless, ᶜAbd al-Raḥmān's sudden death may have simplified matters a little. The date of his death is variously given as 53, 55, or 56. But since he is also said to have died a year before Aishah, the last date, which fits well with the above episode, is to be preferred.[44] Whether his passing-away had anything to do with Aishah's friendly reception of Muᶜāwiyah when he interviewed her that same year in Medina in connection with this question of succession is difficult to say. She seems to have been informed that Muᶜāwiyah was thinking of taking drastic measures against the leading opposers of his plan. So Aishah first preached him an eloquent sermon, while Muᶜāwiyah insisted that he esteemed these men too highly to kill them. Yet he complained to her of their resistance and pointed out that he and others had already taken the oath of allegiance to Yazīd and that he could not, therefore, revoke that accomplished act. Aishah, no doubt realizing full well that Muᶜāwiyah was determined and prepared to carry out his plans,

[42] *Iṣābah*, II, 980; Nawawī, p. 378.

[43] Ṭabarī, II, 196 f.; Dīnawarī, *Akhbār al-Ṭiwāl*, ed. Vladimir Guirgass (Leiden, 1888), pp. 238 f.; cf. above, pp. 89 f.

[44] *Iṣābah*, II, 980 f.; Nawawī, p. 378; *Aghānī*, XIV, 70.

wisely counseled him to be patient and forbearing, saying these opponents will then do what he desired.[45]

There is one other recorded incident of direct contact between Aishah and Muᶜāwiyah. This involved the sale of Aishah's apartment adjoining the Mosque of the Prophet. The purchaser is said to have been Muᶜāwiyah, though others claim it was her nephew ᶜAbd Allah, who is again said to have "inherited" the apartment from her. This confusion in the records is due to overlooking the fact that Aishah had come to own two of these mosque apartments, since Sawdah (d. 54/674) willed her apartment to her. It is this second apartment that Aishah sold to Muᶜāwiyah for the generous sum of 180,000 or 200,000 dirhams and the right to use the property during her lifetime.[46] This would still leave Aishah her own original apartment, which was probably the one that ᶜAbd Allah bought for so large a sum in cash that it took five camels to transport the purchase money. He too allowed Aishah the use of the property for her lifetime.[47] Lammens sees Muᶜāwiyah's purchase as "disguised generosity."[48] ᶜAbd Allah, however, had no need to disguise any generosity of his to his Aunt Aishah, who continued to live in her apartment and turned it over to him in her will.[49] The "sale," therefore, seems to

[45] Ibn al-Athīr, III, 422; cf. Ibn Qutaibah (pseud.), *Kitāb al-Imāmah wa al-Siyāsah* (Cairo, *s.a.*), I, 133.

[46] Ibn Saᶜd, VIII, 118; Caetani, *Annali dell' Islam* (10 vols.; Milan, 1905–26), I, 379, n. 1; cf. Abū Nuᶜaim, II, 47, 49.

[47] Ibn Saᶜd, *loc. cit.*

[48] "Moᶜâwia Ier," *op. cit.*, p. 138.

[49] Ibn ᶜAsākir, VII, 400, 402.

have been something in the nature of outward competition with Muᶜāwiyah. No date is specified for either sale, though they probably took place during Muᶜāwiyah's last visit to Medina.

There does not seem to have been much of local politics in Medina in which Aishah openly participated. Her influence here was working through other channels, of which more presently. There were, however, a few occasions on which Aishah again came to the fore. One of these was in connection with the death of Ḥasan ibn ᶜAlī, said to have taken place in 49, 50, or 51, but was probably in either 50 or 51, since he died after the execution of Ḥujr ibn ᶜAdī, for whose death the year 50 is the earliest given.[50] Ḥasan had expressed in his last illness a wish to be buried with his grandfather, the prophet Mohammed. Since the latter was buried in Aishah's apartment, her consent was felt necessary before Ḥasan's wish could materialize. His brother Ḥusain is credited with securing this consent, so that, when Ḥasan did die, his body was started on its funeral path to Mohammed's tomb. The procession, however, was interrupted by Marwān ibn al-Ḥakam and Saᶜīd ibn al-ᶜĀṣ (who was then the governor of Medina) on the grounds that such a burial would lead to civil war. It is easy enough to understand why these two, representing Umayyad interests, would oppose such a burial. For it would tend to surround this son of ᶜAlī with the same halo

[50] Ṭabarī, II, 143, 144; III, 2323 f.; Ibn al-Athīr, III, 383; Yaᶜqūbī, II, 267; cf. above, p. 193.

that surrounded Mohammed, Abū Bakr, and ᶜUmar, all three of whose mortal remains rested in that hallowed spot in Aishah's house which itself was in the sacred Mosque of the Prophet. But it is difficult to see Aishah in the first place granting her permission for such a burial. Another version of the episode seems to be more in keeping with Aishah's general outlook. According to this, Aishah, riding a gray she-mule, came out to meet the funeral procession protesting: "This is my house. I do not grant permission to anyone (to be buried) in it." There were some disturbances among the record crowd gathered and fear of even worse. Aishah's young nephew Qāsim, the son of Mohammed ibn Abī Bakr, came to her and said, "O Aunt, we have not washed our heads (that is, done with or recovered) from the Battle of the Red Camel, do you wish to have people speak of the Battle of the Gray Mule?" So she returned to her home. Presently, thanks to Marwān and Saᶜīd, the funeral procession headed for the Moslem cemetery of Baqīᶜ.[51]

Another public incident at Medina in which Aishah figured prominently was again a funeral, this time that of Saᶜd ibn Abī Waqqāṣ, the prominent Companion who had refused to take any part in the civil wars, and one who held Aishah responsible in part for the death of ᶜUthmān.[52] But in his case, too, as in the case of ᶜAlī and Muᶜāwiyah, Aishah was seemingly willing to forget the past. Saᶜd died most probably in

[51] Yaᶜqūbī, II, 267; Ibn al-Athīr, III, 383.

[52] Cf. above, p. 167.

55, at a place some seven to ten miles out of Medina, but his body was brought to the city for burial.[53] Aishah and the rest of Mohammed's widows asked Saᶜd's relatives to bring the bier to the mosque so that they could pray over it. This was done. The deed, however, roused some criticism, and some objected to taking the corpse to the mosque. Aishah rebuked the objectors and reminded them that Mohammed himself had prayed in the mosque over the corpse of one of the Companions.[54]

On a third occasion, Aishah intervened to insure the just disposition of the estate of her "sister" Ṣafīyah (d. 50 or 52/670 or 672). This widow of Mohammed had willed a third of her large estate to her nephew. But, because the latter was a Jew, there were those who wished to nullify the bequest. Aishah, on being appealed to, sent word to the objectors to honor the will. This the objectors did.[55] Perhaps they were touched by her loyalty to the wishes of a former rival, who had furthermore opposed her in the affair of ᶜUthmān.[56]

Though Aishah's political influence suffered a severe setback in the period under consideration, yet her general position in the Islamic community at large came, in time, to acquire a dignity compatible with her privileged relationship to Mohammed, her own active mind and wide experience, and the respect

[53] Cf. Nawawī, p. 276; *Iṣābah*, II, 162 f.

[54] Ibn Saᶜd, III¹, 104 f.; Ibn Ḥanbal, VI, 169; *Ṣifat al-Ṣafwah*, I, 140.

[55] Ibn Saᶜd, VIII, 92.

[56] Cf. above, p. 122.

due her advanced age. Men and women of all classes came from far and near to this Mother of the Believers to listen, to inquire, and to be guided. Humble men came to ask for her prayers or for her advice on some personal matter, domestic or financial.[57] Distinguished men sought her advice[58] or her company,[59] while the men of Quraish made a special point of calling on her during her visits to Mecca.[60] Women came to hear her traditions or to seek a solution of some perplexing family problem[61] or even to ask for instruction on proper feminine attire and the use of cosmetics.[62]

It is not surprising, therefore, that the long list of names of those who heard and transmitted traditions from her includes those of some of the foremost of early Moslem traditionists.[63] She herself ranks with such leading traditionists of the school of Medina as Abū Hurairah, Ibn ᶜUmar, and Ibn al-ᶜAbbās. She is credited with 2,210 traditions, of which 1,210 are said to have been reported direct from Mohammed.[64] While she may not have been above putting words in

57 *Aghānī*, XXI, 276; Ibn Ḥanbal, VI, 246; Baiḍāwī, *Anwār al-Tanzīl* . . . . , ed. Fleischer (2 vols.; Lipsiae, 1846–48), I, 100.

58 Ibn Saᶜd, VI, 49, 202.

59 *Ibid.*, V, 341 f., 329.

60 *Ibid.*, p. 218; cf. Yāqūt, *Muᶜjam al-Buldān* (*Geog. Dict.*), ed. Wüstenfeld (6 vols.; Leipzig, 1924), II, 228.

61 Ibn Saᶜd, VIII, 358; Ibn Ḥanbal, VI, 272.

62 Ibn Saᶜd, VIII, 49 f., 352, 358; Ibn Ḥanbal, VI, 210.

63 Cf. *Iṣābah*, IV, 694 f.; Nawawī, p. 849.

64 Nawawī, p. 849; cf. Lammens, "Moᶜâwia Ier," *MFOB*, III, 208 f.

Mohammed's mouth when something she deemed important was at stake, the greater probability is that later others, to suit their own purposes, put words into *her* mouth, as they did into the mouths of most of the other leading Companions. That the informed Moslem world was aware of this fruitful source of fabricated traditions is clearly indicated by the actions of the master-compilers of Islamic traditions—Bukhārī and Muslim—who threw overboard a large proportion of the enormous body of traditions they found in circulation. In Aishah's case, for instance, the two accepted as authentic only 174 of the 1,210 traditions she was said to have received direct from Mohammed, while an additional 54 and 68 were accepted separately by Bukhārī and Muslim, respectively.[65]

No doubt the great majority of questions put to Aishah dealt with the supposed utterances of Mohammed and with the details of his life both public and private. It is instructive to note that those interested frequently used Aishah and her closest harem rival in the matter of traditions, Umm Salamah, as a check on and a source of verification of the other's pronouncements.[66] No doubt these two Mothers of the Believers had many an occasion to supplement, if not indeed to contradict, each other's words, particularly where ʿAlī and the members of his family were

[65] Nawawī, p. 849; cf. Ibn Ḥanbal, VI, 29–282, for her *musnad*, or collection of traditions attributed to her.

[66] Cf. Ibn Ḥanbal, VI, 296, 299, 301, 311, and above, pp. 187 f.

involved, since Umm Salamah was decidedly and consistently pro-ᶜAlīd. On such occasions those interested used their own judgments or followed their own inclinations in giving preference to the version of one or the other of the two. There were, however, many matters on which their reports agreed. In the face of such agreement even Abū Hurairah could do no less than concede their superior knowledge,[67] while Ibn al-ᶜAbbas had to act in accordance with their decision.[68] There were, of course, occasions when Aishah alone either took it upon herself or else was called on to confirm or deny traditions repeated by others. She, on one occasion, corrected Ibn ᶜUmar, who accepted the correction in silence.[69] This same Ibn ᶜUmar once led his fellow-traditionist, Abū Hurairah, by the hand to Aishah to seek her confirmation or denial of a tradition transmitted by the latter. She, on that occasion, confirmed the tradition reported by Abū Hurairah.[70] But on another she accused him of repeating what he had indeed not heard, whereupon Abū Hurairah replied that, while he sought traditions, she busied herself with her toilet.[71]

Aishah was no doubt familiar with many a revelation of Mohammed, particularly those that had any bearing on the harem. The claim, however, that she

[67] Ibn Ḥanbal, VI, 312.

[68] Nawawī, p. 387.

[69] Ibn Ḥanbal, VI, 55; Bukhārī, *Ṣaḥiḥ*, ed. Krehl (4 vols.; Leiden, 1862–1908), I, 443 f.; Ṭabarī, I, 1765 f.

[70] Ibn Saᶜd, IV², 57 f.

[71] *Ibid.*, II², 119; *Iṣābah*, IV, 394.

had memorized all his revelations—that is, the entire Qurʾān—during his lifetime is an attempt of later enthusiasts to add to the religious and intellectual stature of the by then sacred Aishah, who in her lifetime never learned to write, though she could, it is stated, read.[72] There are some traditions, originating with Aishah herself, that indicate a limited knowledge on her part of the Qurʾānic text in this period of her life. In relating the story of the scandal about her and the young Ṣafwān, she reported how she misquoted a Qurʾānic verse and added by way of an explanation of her error of omission that she was then but a young girl and had not yet read or recited much of the Qurʾān.[73] On another occasion she stated how they (i.e., the women in the harem) used to observe the regulations imposed by a new revelation without, however, memorizing its text.[74] The very few occasions on which Aishah is reported to have made some slight corrections in the ʿUthmānic text[75] is in keeping with these statements of hers. There are, on the other hand, ample indications that later Aishah, like

[72] Balādhurī, *Futūḥ*, p. 472.

[73] Bukhārī, III, 107; Wāqidī, *Kitāb al-Maghāzī*, trans. Wellhausen (Berlin, 1882), p. 187; cf. above, p. 35.

[74] *ʿIqd*, I, 209.

[75] Ibn Ḥanbal, VI, 73, 95, 178; Dānī, *Muqniʿ*, ed. Otto Pretzl (Istanbul, 1932), pp. 126–29; Nöldeke *et al.*, *Geschichte des Qorâns* (2d ed.; Leiden, 1937), II, 47, 53 f., 163 (n. 2); Ignácz Goldziher, *Die Richtungen der islamischen Koranauslegung* (Leiden, 1920), pp. 14, 27, 32, 35, 50 (n. 2); Jeffery, *Materials for the History of the Text of the Qurʾān* (Leiden, 1937), pp. 231–33 and, for Arabic text, pp. 83–85.

Ḥafṣah and Umm Salamah, had her own copy or copies of the Qurʾānic text—presumably the standard ᶜUthmānic text.[76] That she was familiar with a good deal, if not all, of its contents is to be deduced from her ready citation of Qurʾānic verses both in her public speeches and in her private conversations.

Aishah's excellent memory stood her in good stead also in the field of poetry, as has been shown in connection with many an incident recorded above. Though no creative poetess herself, she nevertheless had the true Arab's passion for that nation's then favorite mode of literary expression. Her familiarity with the nation's storehouse of poetry and her ready use of it excited the admiration of her listeners.[77] It was no doubt a factor in that eloquence for which she was so widely famed.[78] She seems, likewise, to have absorbed and retained much of her father's knowledge of Arab history and genealogy.[79] Among her intellectual gifts were included also some practical knowledge of medicine[80] and astronomy.[81]

These sizable gifts helped Aishah to create and maintain for herself a unique position in the Islamic

[76] See references in preceding note.

[77] Cf., e.g., *Aghānī*, III, 13; XV, 141; *ᶜIqd*, I, 105, 232; *Iṣābah*, IV, 693; *Ṣifat al-Ṣafwah*, II, 16.

[78] Cf. above, p. 184.

[79] *Ṣifat al-Ṣafwah*, II, 16; Abū Nuᶜaim, II, 49 f.; cf. Bukhārī, III, 427, for her discourse on pre-Islamic marriage customs.

[80] See preceding note and *Iṣābah*, IV, 693.

[81] *Aghānī*, X, 60; see below, p. 208.

community. Her effective use of them laid the foundation for a series of progressively exaggerated estimates of her intellectual abilities. Orthodox Islam conceded her first the honor of being superior in knowledge to any other Mother of the Believers and then to all of them collectively. Soon her great knowledge was reported to have exceeded that of all other women put together. Finally she came to be considered among the wisest and most knowing of all people.[82]

II

Aishah's considerable public activities of this period were not allowed to crowd out her active interest in the affairs of the different members of the family of Abū Bakr. Despite a few family quarrels and some differences of opinion, she continued to watch out for their general welfare and personal happiness at the same time that she stood ready to defend any one of her brothers or sisters, nephews or nieces, against any sort of attack from without.

Already related is the part that Aishah played in preventing the marriage of her young sister, Umm Kulthūm, to the caliph ʿUmar.[83] It was most probably she who eventually arranged this sister's marriage to Ṭalḥah. After the latter's fall in the Battle of the Camel, Aishah once more took the now widowed

[82] *Iṣābah*, IV, 692 f.; *Ṣifat al-Ṣafwah*, II, 15 f.; Abū Nuʿaim, II, 49 f.

[83] See above, pp. 91–93.

Umm Kulthūm under her protective wing. Umm Kulthūm later remarried, but the sisterly bond between the two continued strong enough for her to comply with Aishah's request to suckle a grandson of ʿUmar so as to make of him a foster-relative who could, therefore, visit Aishah freely.[84]

Aishah's interest extended to the children of Umm Kulthūm and Ṭalḥah. She watched over the proper conduct of their youthful son, Zakariyā,[85] and came to the rescue of their daughter—and her own namesake—Aishah. This younger Aishah resembled her distinguished aunt in more than one respect. Unhampered by the restrictions placed upon the older Aishah as Mother of the Believers, this Aishah bint Ṭalḥah lived a high life and achieved distinction in the brilliant social circles of her day. For it was she who competed with Sukainah, the granddaughter of ʿAlī, for the first social position of the Meccan aristocracy. Both women were wealthy in their own right and both freely patronized the singers and poets of that still gay period in early Islam. Their admiring contemporaries, perhaps not wishing to play favorites, came to refer to the two rival women as the "two pearls of Quraish."[86] These beautiful and brilliant society ladies were much sought after in marriage. It was one of the distinctions of Muṣʿab ibn al-Zubair,

[84] Ibn Saʿd, VIII, 338 f.; cf. above, pp. 27–29.

[85] Ibn Saʿd, VIII, 99, 338.

[86] Ibn Khallikān, II, 200; cf. Abbott, "Women and the State in Early Islam," *JNES*, I (1942), 347 f., 351, 363 f.

full brother to ᶜAbd Allah and, therefore, nephew and first cousin to the elder and younger Aishah, respectively, that he won both Sukainah and Aishah to wife.[87]

The elder Aishah had arranged her young niece's first marriage to the girl's cousin, ᶜAbd Allah, the son of ᶜAbd al-Raḥmān ibn Abī Bakr. This marriage, however, does not seem to have been a happy one, for at one time the two separated, and the younger Aishah went to live with her aunt, who disapproved of these doings and four months later brought about a reconciliation between the young couple.[88] It was this niece who in later years attributed her own remarkable knowledge of the stars to the instruction of her Aunt Aishah.[89]

It seems to have been Aishah's policy to arrange marriages between her nieces and nephews. For again it was she who, in the absence of her brother, ᶜAbd al-Raḥmān, arranged for the marriage of his daughter Ḥafṣah to Mundhir, son of Zubair and Asmā bint Abī Bakr. ᶜAbd al-Raḥmān, on his return, resented Aishah's action, though the arrangement was allowed to stand.[90]

Aishah and ᶜAbd al-Raḥmān had another family quarrel. This was over the matter of the care and rearing of the orphaned children of their murdered

[87] Balādhurī, *Ansāb*, V (Jerusalem, 1936), 282–85, 345; *Aghānī*, III, 103 f., 122, 170–72.

[88] *Aghānī*, X, 56.

[89] *Ibid.*, p. 60.

[90] Ibn Saᶜd, VIII, 344; Mālik, *Muwaṭṭā*ᵓ (Cairo, A.H. 1339), II, 37 f.

brother Mohammed. ʿAbd al-Raḥmān, who was on the scene when Mohammed was murdered, was able to rescue the latter's children—a boy named Qāsim and a girl, Quraibah—and to take them with him from Egypt to Medina. Both ʿAbd al-Raḥmān and Aishah wished to keep the youngsters. Aishah won out, but the incident created a strained situation between her and her brother. As Qāsim later told the story, Aishah's motive in this case was her determination to spare the helpless children any possible ill-treatment at the hands of any of the several wives of ʿAbd al-Raḥmān. Qāsim bore loving and grateful testimony to the care and affection that Aunt Aishah lavished on him and his sister. When the children were grown and able to help themselves, she yielded them to ʿAbd al-Raḥmān.[91]

ʿAbd al-Raḥmān died suddenly and away from home, but not far from Mecca, to which city he was taken for burial. Here came Aishah to mourn in the words of the poet at the tomb of her oldest, though last-surviving, and only full brother.[92]

References have already been made to numerous incidents testifying to the close relationship that existed between Aishah and her nephew ʿAbd Allah ibn al-Zubair. However, there is recorded one instance of a serious rift between them. The reason for this was financial, though its exact nature is not easy to deter-

[91] *Aghānī,* XXI, 14 f.; for the girl's name cf. Suyūṭī, *Lub al-Albāb*, ed. Veth (Lugduni Batavorum, 1840), p. 206.

[92] *Aghānī,* XIV, 70; *Iṣābah,* II, 980 f.

mine. It seems that Aishah either disposed of some property or funds as gifts or allowances or else sold some of her property (to Muᶜāwiyah?)[93] under circumstances that either displeased or alarmed ᶜAbd Allah. He, on hearing of the transaction, is reported to have said that he would certainly have to prohibit these activities of Aishah if she herself did not cease from them. His words were carried to Aishah, who in turn swore not to speak to ᶜAbd Allah as long as she lived. A considerable length of time passed; but Aishah still insisted on keeping her oath. She turned down all pleas on behalf of ᶜAbd Allah, whom she refused to see. Finally, aided by some friends, he gained access to her presence by a ruse. These peacemaking friends, together with ᶜAbd Allah, presented themselves before her apartment and asked to see her. She bid them to enter. "All of us?" they asked.

"Yes, all of you," said Aishah, not suspecting ᶜAbd Allah's presence. Brought together again, there was much tearful pleading to end the unhappy affair. Aishah finally yielded. But in speaking to ᶜAbd Allah she broke the oath she had formerly taken; to ease her conscience on that score, she manumitted forty slaves.[94]

These references to probable sales of property executed by Aishah may indicate that she traded in real estate, though on what scale it would be hard to say.

[93] See above, pp. 197 f.

[94] Bukhārī, IV, 129 f.; Ibn Ḥanbal, IV, 327 f.; Abū Nuᶜaim, II, 49; *Ṣifat al-Ṣafwah*, II, 14; cf. Bukhārī, I, 383.

There are also some references to her trading in slaves. But again it is difficult to say if this was only for her domestic needs or primarily for profit, as some seem to think.[95] For, in carrying on a business of her own, Aishah would be doing no more and no less than many an aristocratic Arab woman of her day. However, the forty slaves she is said to have freed in the above incident were bought expressly for that occasion.[96] Again the number forty may be a later exaggeration aimed at increasing Aishah's reputation for piety and good deeds, since the liberation of a slave was considered a great merit. Aishah, while yet a young wife to Mohammed, indulged on several occasions in this form of charity.[97] There were also instances where she promised her personal slaves their freedom following her own death.[98] A curious story is told of how a girl slave who was so promised her freedom cast a death spell over Aishah so as to hasten the day of her own liberation. A "doctor" visiting in Medina pronounced the sick Aishah not really sick but certainly bewitched. The slave confessed. The generous Aishah took no other step against her than to order her sold and replaced by another.[99]

Aside from Aishah's political, domestic, and busi-

[95] E.g., Dermenghem, *Life of Mahomet*, trans. Arabella Yorke (London, 1930), p. 286, where, however, his sources are not mentioned.

[96] Abū Nuᶜaim, II, 49.

[97] Bukhārī, I, 29 f.; Ibn Ḥanbal, VI, 135; Ibn al-Athīr, II, 209, 266.

[98] E.g., Ibn Saᶜd, V, 218; VIII, 53.

[99] Ibn Ḥanbal, VI, 40; but see Dermenghem, *op. cit.*, p. 286.

ness affairs, what, one may ask, was the color or tone of her own inner life in this period? Many are the references in the traditions to her God-fearing and prayerful life, as seen in both her acts and her words. She was given, it seems, to the tearful reading of the Qurʾān and to long periods of fasting and prayers.[100] She is credited, for instance, with a statement which is freely interpreted to mean that it matters not if one is blamed or praised, for what really counts is whether one is himself blame- or praiseworthy.[101] Or, again, asked when a man is a sinner, she is said to have replied, "When he supposes that he is righteous."[102]

Equally numerous are the traditions that bear witness to the almost ascetic simplicity of her life. Not a few add or imply that she could not bear to live in comfort, let alone luxury, as long as she remembered the hardships and poverty of Mohammed's life[103] or recalled his personal advice to her to content herself with little of this world's goods—a traveler's provisions and old clothes—and to beware of the company of the wealthy.[104] She, therefore, wore patched clothes and on occasion rebuked the Companions of the prophet for their high living and extravagant attire.[105] Her own resources, which were varied in

[100] E.g., *Ṣifat al-Ṣafwah*, V, 14 f.; Abū Nuᶜaim, II, 47–49.

[101] *ᶜIqd*, I, 221; II, 89.

[102] Cf. Margaret Smith, *An Early Mystic of Baghdad* (London, 1935), pp. 137, 273.

[103] E.g., Ibn Saᶜd, I², 114.

[104] *Ibid.*, VIII, 52 f.

[105] *Ibid.*, I², 117 f.; *ᶜIqd*, I, 394.

source and considerable in size, she is said to have dispersed largely in charity.[106] But similar stories of such extravagant charity are told also of some of the other Mothers of the Believers.[107] At any rate, with Aishah, charity began at home; and "home" to her included her paternal and maternal clans.[108] Her nephew ᶜAbd Allah ibn al-Zubair, who was, as has already been seen, also her "son" and "heir," is said to have contrasted the manner of her great liberality with that of his likewise generous mother, Asmā. The latter lost no time in distributing what was ready to hand. Aishah, on the other hand, accumulated what she received into large quantities or sums before she distributed them to good advantage.[109]

But careful examination of all the sources leads one to conclude that Aishah neither stinted herself on worldly goods nor allowed her piety to curtail her social freedom. Wisely, she took the middle path of life and observed, for the most part, the accepted proprieties. She was, thus, neither as "progressive" as, for instance, her own niece Aishah, nor as "conservative" as her "sister" Umm Salamah. Starting with the obvious temperance and moderation of this period of her life, the Moslem traditions came in time to draw a picture of an ascetic and devout Aishah whose guiding principle in life was to live in the faith, hope for its

[106] E.g., Ibn Saᶜd, VIII, 45 f., 118.

[107] *Ibid.*, pp. 46, 77 f.; Ibn Ḥanbal, VI, 121.

[108] See, e.g., Ṭabari, I, 3096.

[109] Nawawī, p. 824; *Ṣifat al-Ṣafwah*, II, 31.

rewards, and practice freely its charities. She accordingly came to be ranked high not only among the sages but also among the saints of orthodox Islam.[110]

But what of Aishah's own pride in herself or of her final estimate of the worth-whileness of her life? The traditions list, as a rule, ten privileges which she claimed distinguished her from the rest of Mohammed's wives, and on which she is said to have openly and freely prided herself. These were that she was the only virgin wife of Mohammed; that both her parents were emigrants; that Allah himself had declared her innocence; that Gabriel had revealed her likeness to Mohammed and instructed him to marry her; that she had washed in the same vessel as did Mohammed; that Mohammed had prayed in her company; that he had received his revelations in her presence; that he had died in her arms; that he had passed away on the night allotted to her; and that he was buried in her house.[111] She is also said to have prided herself on being the best beloved of Mohammed, the well-born and trustworthy daughter of the trustworthy Abū Bakr, and on being one who was promised (by Allah) forgiveness and reward.[112]

The points, then, in which Aishah took special personal pride were such as were hers by virtue of either

[110] Cf., e.g., Abū Nuᶜaim, II, 43 ff.; *Ṣifat al-Ṣafwah*, II, 14 f.; see also Margaret Smith, *Rābiᶜa the Mystic and Her Fellow Saints in Islam* (Cambridge, 1928), p. 4.

[111] Ibn Saᶜd, VIII, 43 f.; *Iṣābah*, IV, 694.

[112] *Iṣābah*, IV, 694; Nawawī, p. 849.

her birth, the love of Mohammed, or the grace of Allah. Furthermore, they refer, for the most part, to that earlier and by far the happiest part of her life as the young and beloved wife of Mohammed. If Aishah, in retrospect, took any personal pride in the momentous undertaking of the second and stormy period of her career, or if she derived any real satisfaction from this third and twilight period of her life, then the orthodox traditions have passed over these facts in silence.

As her last illness (nature not stated) overtook her, Aishah realized that the end was at hand, and she would not be persuaded otherwise.[113] She gave a few directions regarding some details of her funeral. There were some who spoke of burying her in her own apartment near Mohammed. This Aishah expressly forbade, saying she wished instead to be buried with the rest of her "sisters."[114] Her reasons for not wishing to be placed near Mohammed are stated in general and vague terms. According to some, it seems that Aishah felt she had lost in the qualities of purity or righteousness since Mohammed's own departure.[115] According to others, her reason was that she had originated an evil innovation after him[116]—which could be interpreted as referring to the civil war with

[113] Ibn Saᶜd, VIII, 53.

[114] Ibn Qutaibah, *Kitāb al-Maᶜārif*, ed. Wüstenfeld (Göttingen, 1850), p. 66; ᶜ*Iqd*, II, 283.

[115] Ibn Qutaibah, *Maᶜārif*, p. 66; Ibn Saᶜd, VIII, 51.

[116] ᶜ*Iqd*, II, 283.

ᶜAlī. According to still others, she shrank from being considered as of great purity or righteousness[117]—as burial near the prophet would imply. Taking the collective evidence of these traditions, the dying Aishah is seen as one who was aware of her shortcomings, sincerely regretted them, and sought, above all things, to escape the great sin of self-righteousness.[118]

As one reads the various accounts of her illness and death, one is struck by the absence of any joyous note of spiritual victory or of heavenly anticipation. Informed that ᶜAbd Allah ibn al-ᶜAbbās asked permission to see her, she replied that she had no need of either him or his praises. Urged by one or more of her nephews to let this righteous "son" take earthly leave of her, she reluctantly received him. In his efforts to comfort her, Ibn al-ᶜAbbās enumerated several of the ten or more of her distinctions already referred to, pointed out how Allah had used various incidents of her life for the benefit of the believers, and dwelt on her approaching reunion with Mohammed. Her response was to wish she had sunk or could sink into complete oblivion.[119] Some traditionists leave this dismal note out,[120] while others seek to explain its several variations by seeing in them Aishah's way of repentance.[121] Some of these variations are that she wished she were a leaf or a tree uttering praises and so

[117] Bukhārī, IV, 434.

[118] Cf. above, p. 212.

[119] Ibn Saᶜd, VIII, 51 f.; Ibn Ḥanbal, I, 276, 349; Bukhārī, III, 297 f.

[120] Bukhārī, III, 297 f.

[121] Ibn Saᶜd, VIII, 51.

fulfilling its obligation; or that she were a plant of the plants of the earth and not anything remembered; or, again, that she were a stone or a lump of clay.[122] Then there are the versions that report her as saying that she wished Allah had not created her as anything at all or that she wished she had not been created.[123] That is, the dying Aishah wished she had never been born. Did this pathetic last wish of the beloved of Mohammed and the Mother of the Believers spring indeed from a deep and religious sense of her own unworthiness as the traditions that paint her also as sage and saint would seem to imply? Or did it not, instead, well up from a weary soul tragically disappointed in *life?*

Aishah passed away on Tuesday, the seventeenth of Ramadān, of the Year 58 (July 13, 678),[124] aged some sixty-four years. Of the widows of Mohammed, she was survived by Umm Salamah, and perhaps also by Maimūnah.[125] Her burial, which took place that night, was attended by one of the largest and most impressive crowds ever gathered until then in the City of the Prophet. Abū Hurairah, then acting governor of Medina, pronounced the last prayers over the body. Her "son," ᶜAbd Allah ibn al-Zubair, and his brother, ᶜUrwah, were among the nephews and grandnephews that performed the last rites of the chief mourners at the grave. She was laid to her final rest,

[122] *Ibid.* [123] *Ibid.*, pp. 51 f. [124] Cf. *EI*, I, 217.

[125] Abū Nuᶜaim, II, 44; Ṭabarī, III, 2437 ff., esp. pp. 2444 and 2453 f.; *Iṣābah,* IV, 795.

there in the company of her departed "sisters," in the cemetery of Baqīᶜ.[126]

III

Aishah's dying wish for complete oblivion was not one to be granted her. Down through the centuries the orthodox Sunni Moslems have continued to sing her praises and to honor her memory, at the same time that heterodox sects, particularly Shīᶜites or followers of ᶜAlī, have continued to invoke public curses on her in the company of the distinguished trio—Abū Bakr, ᶜUmar, and ᶜUthmān. The West, in general, has shown a mild interest in her romantic relationship to Mohammed. Orientalists, who have paid her somewhat closer attention, have at times classed her with the Agrippinas and Elizabeths of history.[127] Today she bids fair to live anew, perhaps even more vividly than she has ever lived before, in the hearts and minds of an ever increasing number of men and women of East and West.

[126] Ibn Saᶜd, VIII, 53 f.

[127] Cf. D. S. Margoliouth, *Mohammed and the Rise of Islam* (London, 1927), p. 450.

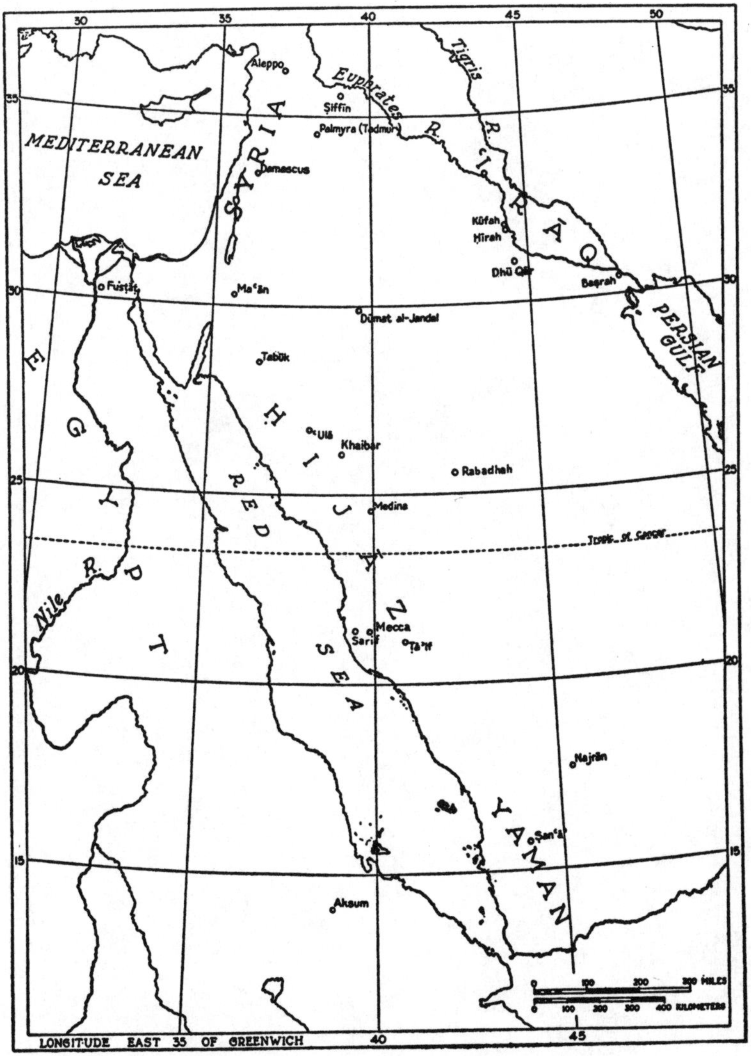

ARABIA AND SURROUNDING LANDS

Index